THE DEEP MURMUR

Preceded by Elegy for Enoch Powell

THE DEEP MURMUR

Preceded by Elegy for Enoch Powell

Renaud Camus

Translated by Ethan Rundell

VAUBAN
BOOKS

Front cover illustration, Renaud Camus, *Château dans le brouillard*. Cover and Interior Design: Robert Kern, TIPS Publishing Services

Library of Congress Control Number: 2024934130

ISBN 979-8-9887399-1-3 (paperback)

Vauban Books
P.O. Box 508
Blowing Rock, NC, 28605
www.vaubanbooks.com

27 26 25 24   1 2 3 4

Contents

Note on The Text

"Elegy for Enoch Powell" first appeared in untitled preface to La Nouvelle Librairie edition of Powell's "Rivers of Blood" speech. See *Discours des fleuves de sang*, preface by Renaud Camus, introduction by Jean-Yves Le Gallou (Les Éditions de la Nouvelle Librairie, Paris, 2019). "The Word 'Race'" and "The Deep Murmur" were published jointly in a volume that, as here, takes its title from the latter. See Renaud Camus, *Le Profond Murmure* (Les Éditions de la Nouvelle Librairie, Paris, 2022).

Elegy for Enoch Powell

I am greatly honored to be invited to preface this rightly famous speech, the prescience and courage of which cannot be overstated.* And I am delighted for the opportunity it presents to pay homage to one of the intellectual and historic figures I admire most, Enoch Powell, a hero of the Second World War and the fight against Nazism, an opponent of appeasement from the start, and, would you believe it, one of only two members of the British Army to have begun the war as a simple soldier and ended it as a general (the youngest ever at the time of his appointment); a poet, linguist, eminent scholar, expert in classical literature and philology, specialist of Herodotus and Thucydides, prominent politician, and great visionary.

It was not, I admit, without a little mischievous provocation that I dedicated my own book, *Le Grand Remplacement*,[1] to two Prophets: the Frenchman, Jean Raspail, and the Englishman, Enoch Powell. Around the same time, now roughly a half-century ago, these two men, each in his own idiom and thanks to the means made available to him by his condition in life, sought to warn the world, the West, Europe, France, England of the looming horror in which we are today plunged—one by way of fiction, as a novelist, with his brilliantly prophetic novel, *The Camp of the Saints*, the

---

* [ed.: Powell's speech is included in appendix to this volume. See pp. 53–56]

1

other as a political orator, with his no less inspired speech, "Rivers of Blood." Neither of them was heeded or even heard. Almost the only thing fictional about the Frenchman's novel, which prevented nothing, was that it was a few decades ahead of the curve, leaving its author today in despair vis-à-vis a turn of events he foretold and with hardly anything to ease his pain, which is the same as mine, other than his faith and a cosmogonic conception of the designs of Providence. As for the Englishman, his speech shattered his career and destroyed the man.

It is with poetic license that this short, epoch-making speech is referred to as "Rivers of Blood." It is vivid and lovely in a tragic sort of way. Yet the expression is not to be found in the speech itself. Powell himself more prosaically referred to this piece of high eloquence as his "Birmingham Speech" (20 April 1968). The name under which it has come down to us stems from a discreet reference to Virgil, who for his part is also not named. The orator speaks of his foreboding at what, *like the Roman*, he discerns. *Like the Roman* was to be the title of his outsized biography, written by Simon Heffer and published by Faber & Faber in 2008.

The image that so caught people's attention was a passing allusion, never revisited, to two verses from the Aeneid, which occur in a sinister flourish by the Cumaean sibyl in Book VI of the epic, 86–87:

Bella, horrida bella,
Et Thybrim multo spumanten sangui cerno.

Jacques Delille translated it thus, in 1804:

Je vois, je vois la guerre et le meurtre et la rage
Et le Tibre effrayé débordant de carnage[*]

---

[*] [ed.: In J.W. Mackail's 1885 translation, which would have been familiar to Powell, these verses are rendered as follows: "Wars, grim wars I discern, and

It is rather odd that this dramatic vignette remains the speech's emblem, as it were, and ultimately even gave it its name, for, as a cultivated man of another time addressing an audience that he supposed capable of grasping his references, Powell very quickly moved on from this alarming evocation. Some do not hesitate to claim, what's more, that this image is false, which according to them would contradict the entire speech and the validity of its prediction: fifty years have passed, they stress, and there have still been no rivers of blood. And it is true that there have been no rivers of blood up till now but nothing, alas, proves these rivers have said their last word. There have indeed been no rivers of blood but there have been many bloody attacks perpetrated by the occupier, hostages executed, in short, and above all, above all, there have been countless little streams, murders, rapes, forced confinements, kidnappings, and all this *nocence*, as I like to say, this relentless determination to harm, to trouble, to ruin life, which has transformed one of Earth's most peaceful and civilized countries, Great Britain, and with it so many others in Europe—Sweden, the Netherlands, Belgium, France, Germany—into chaotic assortments of untidy and dilapidated wastelands, brutish and ultraviolent, which everyday put us on notice, in public transportation, in hospitals, in schools, in the street, as to their status as pioneering outposts of the global shanty town.

There have been no rivers of blood, no, but this is because England, which displayed such exemplary heroism, such unparalleled steadfastness, such spirit of resistance faced with previous threats of invasion, has this time extraordinarily seen to its own submission; a submission not so much, if at all, to the invaders themselves as to the forces, and mechanisms, and interests that have brought them in ever greater numbers, that have imposed them and that protect them. Had he been confronted with this

Tiber afoam with streams of blood." See J.W. Mackail, *The Aeniad of Virgil*, Macmillan and Co. (London, 1885), p. 122.]

terrible choice, submission or war, I am not sure that Powell would not have preferred war, a war which in this instance would have had nothing civil about it, the decolonial uprising of the natives, their revolt against the genocidal, ethnocidal governments, that he would not have preferred this, I was saying, to the constant humiliation of his people, to its headlong disappearance from ever greater areas of the territory, to its present status as a minority in the very capital of its kingdom, under a Muslim mayor with a veiled wife. What is happening is in fact yet worse, uglier, baser, dirtier, more foolish, sadder, infinitely less glorious, and less *English* than what he had foretold and which was already so frightening.

It is true that, when it was given, the speech caused an enormous scandal, but it was also generally well-received by the public, at least among the native population. The orator received thousands of letters and telegrams, the vast majority of which were enthusiastic, and which thanked him for his courage. It was the politicking and media class, first and foremost the establishment of his own Conservative Party, that saw to it that no heed be paid these powerful and vividly expressed warnings, and that forever shattered Powell's career—he had defied a power greater than he.

I am not thinking of the invader here. The invader is countless in number, it is true, but not so much so that a determined people—and God knows the English can be determined when they put their minds to it—would be incapable of overcoming him without too much trouble. Even today, when the process of colonization is twenty or thirty times more advanced than when the following speech was given, even today it remains entirely possible to liberate the national territory by means of remigration or repatriation, duly mentioned by Powell. But he was dealing with an opponent quite other than the colonist or occupier, far more powerful than him because shapeless and faceless, indeed without attributable existence, nameless, with no other will than that of the machine or algorithm, a pure tropism.

For, like the triangular trade before it, the present-day colonization of Europe has *three* protagonists, not two. There are those who *do* it or *are* it: the immigrants, the migrants, the "refugees," the conquerors, the colonists, the occupier. There are those who are subjected to it, willingly or no: the natives and assimilated, the autochthones, the colonized, the subjected, the conquered, the occupied. And there are those who want it or propel it, who drive it forward without even having to want it via the operation of mere mechanical, legal, verbal, accounting, and financial linkages: political staffers, journalists, judges, the world of finance, employers, the European Union in its present form, the IMF, the UN, Facebook, Twitter, Google, Amazon, and so on. In the Great Replacement now underway there are the replacers, the replacees, and the replacists. And the replacists are themselves the unlikely combination of two forces that one would have thought as remote from one another as possible, whose foot soldiers do not always even know that they are allied, but whose interests are in fact highly complementary and convergent, to such a point that the cordial relations between them, what one might call their objective alliance, to use the vocabulary of another era, have up till now rendered them invincible, all-powerful. I am here of course referring to profit and the search for profit, on the one hand, the purely managerial conception of the world and the management of the human park (Sloterdijk), economism, financialization, Davos, and *davocracy*, this administration of the world by Great Financiers, banks, multinationals, robots, business, Big Tech; and, on the other, antiracism or, more specifically, the *second* antiracism, the one that is no longer, like the first, the necessary and eminently moral protection of a few threatened races, but the hatred of all, the pseudo-scientific negation of their existence and the desire to eradicate them, to suppress all differences between them, to merge them. And not just races but now also sexes and, while it is at it, nations, cultures, civilizations—all that separates and distinguishes, all that lends itself to discrimination, all that harms the mass production of the new man, of Nutella-man, of surimi-humanity, of Undifferentiated Human Material (UHM), infinitely exchangeable, spreadable at will, a paste without lumps or clots, pressed by the press and ground down by the courts, liquified (Bauman), ready-made for every shanty of the global shantytown, this shanty universe wherein reigns the copy, the reproduction, the imitation, the ersatz, the low-cost, the fake, the inverted real, the *faussel,*[*] mass negationism: where what is happening is not happening.

To prevent the Powells, the Raspails, and all the unfortunates who have followed in their footsteps from being heard even though they are merely stating the obvious, there is this fearsome, almost unprecedented coalition—even if, in Rome, financiers and speculators were already skilled at stirring up the plebians *and all that vomits Subure and Ergastule*[2] against the Republic and even against the people itself. I mean the coalition of interests that one traditionally describes as "rightwing," because they are those of the propertied, the landowners, the employers (profit, trade, exchange, deregulation, rising consumption on the basis of demographic growth), and what are or were once usually seen as "leftwing" ideals and "values" (antiracism, equality, the freedom of movement). As soon as the product is man himself, at once producer (less and less thanks to machines), consumer (more and more), and product ("if you're not paying for the product, you are the product"), there is no longer any conflict between the free circulation of merchandise, so dear to finance and trade, and the free circulation of individuals, so dear to antiracist egalitarianism. And not only does this fusion of rightwing interests and leftwing ideals render invincible the unprecedented power that embodies and carries it out

---

[*]   [ed.: A neologism. Camus defines the *faussel* as "the inverted real, the real false, the false real." Even when its untruth is patent, the *faussel,* by sheer repetition, can achieve a kind of second-order reality, purely discursive and non-representational. It at once travesties reality and comes to substitute for it.]

(global replacism, planetary davocracy), not only does it allow it to invent the news every morning, by selection and rejection, but it also makes it sympathetic, morally irreproachable, impossible to criticize: even if there is nothing there but an industrial process for obtaining an ever more homogenous and chemically pure spread, who would dare rise up against antiracism and the equality of man, the equality of man and woman, of heirs and non-heirs, etc.?

Along the way, this fusion between hyperclass and hyper-antiracism supplies the resulting planetary power with its auxiliary militias and volunteer thugs, its hooligans[3], its antifa and other black bloc hordes, who think they are fighting capitalism while performing the greatest services for hypercapitalism, first by wielding violence and threats to hound the opponents of the global shantytown and the factories of Undifferentiated Human Matter (UHM), next by breaking everything as soon as the opportunity presents itself, which helps grease the wheels of trade and consumption—harming small shopkeepers, no doubt, but helping large retailers. In times past, rich kids who adopted ultra-leftist positions seemed to be commendably acting against their own class interests, and this was ascribed to a generational paradox, even as it was assumed that these young people would end up becoming notaries, ministers, new philosophers,[4] and reliable clients of the talk-show circuit; today, the same young people, even if they do not realize it, directly serve the industries of man and those who finance them, with the result that everything is back to normal, their parents can be proud of them.

Negationism and genocide have made great strides since the last time round, above all in the domain of public relations, there where they least excelled in the past. Aided by an army of efficient press secretaries, they have very successfully endeavored to forge a better image for themselves. They wasted no time in digesting and implementing the essential message of their online consultants: to wit, that if one is to follow through with a crime without unduly causing protest and even enjoy the support of public opinion, international bodies, and the pope, that crime should be perpetrated *in the name of good* and not *in the name of evil*. A genocide that does not earn you the Nobel Peace Prize or a standing ovation before continental or planetary assemblies is a botched genocide, an amateur genocide, pre-post-industrial. With that aim in view, racism will not get you anywhere in the media. Antiracism, which only provokes sympathy, subsidies, and advances on earnings, starting of course with the most precious and valuable of them all, those of the victims, is a thousand times better.

Another advance, incidentally, is that one may now eliminate without strictly speaking killing, which despite everything always leads to protests, qualms, and defections. It is enough to replace. This method takes a bit longer but is much more reliable. Racism wiped the *shtetl* from the map; antiracism is in the process of finishing off European civilization. And by definition, by nature, by essence, by a supreme effect, one is tempted to write, of the art of public relations, those who are here designated as criminals are not those who commit the crime—to the contrary, *they* find themselves heaped with canned applause in the stupor-producing studios—but rather those who seek to prevent it.

Under these conditions, which were already being put in place in his time, Powell had no chance of being heard. The spectacle he described was in the plain view of everyone and they could only observe the perfect coincidence between his sentences and the facts, between word and thing, between his speech and reality. But it is one thing to see; it is quite another to have seen. In *The Emperor's New Clothes* (the most accurate literary and philosophical metaphor for our situation these past fifty years), the people in its entirety can see that the king is naked but, to say or even think this, each of them would have to admit to being an imbecile to themselves and everyone else. On this point, it is not to be forgotten, ideologues, court sociologists, tailors, and crooks are categorical: imbeciles are the only ones who do not see that the sovereign is dressed in a magnificent outfit of woven gold. Our own fate is even more bitter than that of the emperor's subjects, the impediment even more difficult for us to overcome. Those who see that the king is naked, those who clearly make out what Powell describes, and who observe what he puts forward as plainly as the nose on your face—to wit, mass immigration, migratory tsunami, ethnic submersion, the Great Replacement, genocide by substitution—not only are they morons, as in Andersen's tale; they are monsters, fascists, Nazis, racists, *pariahs*, the socially dead, the living dead. But no one particularly aspires to this uncomfortable status, it goes without saying, whether socially or personally. Better again to not see, possibly in all good faith, and above all to not say. People are in general honest: they abstain from taking too much notice of that for which they have no name. The eye is a rather stupid organ, and above all very lazy, and it hates troubling itself: when the words are lacking and above all not acceptable, it prudently refrains from noticing. *What little Great Replacement with chromed handlebars at the back of the courtyard?*

Since the Birmingham Speech, successive governments have done nothing to put an end to the evils it describes. Nothing has been done to prevent those it foretells. To the contrary, these evils have been worsened a hundred times over. Great civilizations that already had one knee on the ground when these words still echoed are today moribund. The destruction of the Europeans of Europe proceeds apace amidst general indifference, without anyone daring to raise a little finger to prevent it. What can we do? It is not with patience that we must arm ourselves, as we have already too amply observed; it is with courage, indignation, and fury. We have only one weapon at our disposal—the truth. Faced with empires built on deceit, it has in the past shown itself to be all-powerful and this despite its weakness and nudity. Did it not, in the space of a few months and by dint of the slow work of several decades, bring down the Soviet empire from within? So will it overcome the replacist empire, which has so many points in common with it, as indeed with all prison-camp totalitarianisms. But time is running out.

The Word "Race"

Race.

> *To Monsieur,*
> *Monsieur Laurent de Boissieu*
> *Since these questions preoccupy him*
> *What will you say, future races,*
> *If true speech sometimes*
> *Recites to you the adventures*
> *Of our appalling times?*
> —Malherbe

With the word *race*, we leave the field of refinement and enter the minefield. This little brochure is a supplement to the article *race* as it appears in the *Dictionnaire des délicatesses du français contemporain.*[*] At the start of the twenty-first century, it is doubtless the most disputed and hence most discussed word in the French language. The mere fact of pronouncing it or writing it can get one a one-way ticket to the worst Limoges, Guantanamos, or Siberias[1] there are.

---

*[*] Camus, Renaud, *Dictionnaire des délicatesses du français contemporain (I-Z)*, self-published, 2021, 2 vol. The most recent version may be consulted at https://www.renaud-camus.net/librairie/.

First, a very dirty trick was played on it, that of establishing or *deciding*, I do not how it should be put, that what it referred to did not exist. To establish as law that one must not speak of races because race or races have no scientific reality is to doubtless display deep scientific knowledge.[2] I am incapable of judging the matter and, to tell the truth, the question hardly interests me. But it is also and above all to show that one knows nothing about linguistics—and, quite simply, to reveal that one does not understand what a word is. Indeed, one might as well say that unicorns do not exist, or social classes, or myths on the grounds that these things have no scientific basis or are not clearly demarcated from what they are not.

I am for my part persuaded that the fearsome taboo that was placed on the word *race* and that contagiously spread to everything to which it might have referred over the course of its immensely rich, centuries-long history is the decisive element, the node, the inflection point of all recent, modern, contemporary ideological history: the most consequential effect of language, not only for thought and the delimitation of its acceptable, admissible space, beyond which social death begins, but also for history itself and the geography of the world, at least the human one. It is doubtless not this that threw hundreds of millions of men and women (above all *men*, in point of fact) onto the roads and seas, but it is this that rendered what once would have been the natural reaction to this type of upheaval, any serious resistance to this floodtide, any self-confident riposte on the part of thousand-year-old cultures, nations, and civilizations impossible and obsolete. For the interests that demanded that man be exchangeable at will, like a product—that he be interchangeable, replaceable, delocalizable, and so be forthwith delocalized, disaffiliated, de-originated, denationalized—it was essential that this sturdy barrier, race, be brought down; and to prevent it from ever going back up again once it had been brought down, anyone who recalled having ever seen it or who spoke to its past existence had to be criminalized. This was the price of the great mixing of populations, with the extinction that it entailed, over time, for the least numerous, the most expensive, and least popular among them, who by means of this prohibition were rendered entirely incapable of defending a space on Earth for themselves, and indeed deprived of any grounds for opposing it.

It has been said, and is still frequently said, that this major prohibition was associated with the Second World War and the extermination of the Jews of Europe, that, after the death camps, one could no longer speak of *races*. This association is not altogether false, of course, but it is also not entirely accurate; and, above all, it is much less direct than one would have had us believe. It was neither the end of the conflict, nor the discovery of the camps, nor their liberation that brought about the taboo. For roughly thirty years after 1945, the word *race* was widely used in the language, and there was still nothing pejorative associated with it. In the school textbooks of the fifties, it was still taught, with the aid of illustrations, that there existed four races—white, yellow, black, and red; when the children got a little older, this was somewhat fine-tuned but without, as far as I can recall, calling into question the principle of this division. Speaking at a ceremony held on the rue Saint-Guillaume to mark the centenary of the École libre des Sciences-Politiques,[3] the then-president of the Republic, Georges Pompidou, could still twice refer to the French as a *race*: "The shock of the defeat, the extraordinary adventure of General de Gaulle, and doubtless a deep-seated reaction of our race have restored to us our vitality, a certain appetite for risk, and even some ambitions."

And several lines further on: "The second obstacle is doubtless the most formidable. As we know only too well, it has to do with the very character of our race, with this versatility that Caesar had already discerned and used against the Gauls, and which makes it so the French people, a people enamored of peace, quiet, and stability, if ever there was one, periodically and abruptly feel an unexpressed and unbridled need for change, for a change that calls everything into question, not just men, but principles, institutions."

Moreover, like all Frenchmen of his generation, and all Frenchmen of earlier generations, and a few Frenchmen of the following generations, Georges Pompidou had a very natural and not at all self-conscious relationship to the word *race*, since he also wrote, in a text of recollections included in the collection, *Le Désir et le Destin*: "My father and mother deeply belonged to the French race. Hard-working, frugal, believers in merit, in the virtues of the mind, in the qualities of the heart."[4]

Faced with such sentences—and there are a countless number of them, our literature overflows with them—to say that races do not exist and that one must not use that word, which, it is claimed, has no meaning, which corresponds to nothing, to say this is itself entirely without meaning. It could only be meaningful on condition that one understands the term in its most miniscule sense, precisely that which the worst kind of racists gave it; and that the antiracists, to their misfortune and ours, to their success and our disaster, have adopted without the least modification, contenting themselves with simply inverting the value assigned it.

It is worth noting in passing that the mere fact of speaking of a *French race*, as all French people did for centuries, suffices to establish that one is not "racist" in the pseudo-scientific sense of the term or one that relies on a scientific or pseudo-scientific conception of the word *race*. Indeed, for the French, one of the advantages of their race is that it has very few ethnic characteristics. This is why individuals and lineages that are foreign to it have always been able to harmoniously join and merge with it over the course of history. But to appreciate this one must understand *race* in the "French" sense, in the full, linguistic, layered sense, that is, in terms of the entire semantic arc that has been deployed in and through it over the course of the language's history. This is marvelously captured by one of the most beautiful sentences of our literature, that of Bernanos in *La Grande Peur des bien-pensants*: "Alas, around the little French boys huddled together over their notebooks, pen in hand, attentive and sticking out their tongues a little, like around young people drunk from their first outing beneath the flowering chestnut trees in the arms of a young blonde girl, there was in times past that vague and enchanted memory, that dream, that deep murmur in which the race cradles its own."[5]

An *enchanted memory*, a *dream*, a *deep murmur*, this is how race makes itself heard in the depths of the language, and this is what it is. We are here far from George Montandon.[6] And yet this disaster has taken place, unfortunately, and the antiracists, obsessed, and understandably so, as we have just seen, with racists and racism, took this word *race* (naively or as a matter of grand strategy, but in a way that would have untold consequences) in exactly the same, incredibly narrow sense as the racists—in order to draw diametrically opposed conclusions, it is true, but the point of departure was the same, and the outcome is not so far removed as one might imagine.

One observes spiraling evolutions, very much in keeping, by the way, with the precepts of bathmology, the science of levels of language.* The meanings return to the same location, it is true, but *at another level of the spiral*. Or, to put it otherwise: they return to another level of the spiral, but it is *at the same location*, with the same effects. This is true, not only of meanings, of words and their significations, but also of the phenomena themselves, of ideologies and facts. I often give the same example, and fittingly enough it concerns antiracism. Drawing its legitimacy, moral foundation, and ideological power from the genocide of the Jews, born and reborn from the fierce and oh-so-justified *never again!* hurled

---

*   On bathmology, cf. *Roland Barthes par Roland Barthes*, "Écrivains de toujours", Seuil, 1974; and Camus (Renaud), *Buena Vista Park*, Hachette-P.O.L., 1980, Chez l'auteur, 2016; and *Du Sens*, P.O.L., 2002.

against the death camps, over the course of fifty years antiracism ultimately built a society—ours—in which the Holocaust can no longer be taught in many schools and that Jews must flee in their thousands because they are no longer safe. In Berlin itself, it is antiracism that accounts for the presence of hundreds of immigrants or descendants of immigrants who demonstrate to cries of *Death to the Jews!* as in the time of Kristallnacht. To those who not so long ago were still surprised that it was necessary to distinguish between racism and antisemitism, history ultimately supplied a cruel and ironic explanation, as is its wont: it was so that the antiracists could be antisemites, an opportunity they do not often pass up. It is to be wondered whether this adjective, *antiracist*, is not on its way to becoming in polite conversation a code word for *antisemite*, as *Anti-Zionist* has long been and generally remains.

One tells oneself in these circumstances that what is necessary is to bring about—but doing so appears nearly impossible—a final and daring reversal, which would represent, as is often the case, nothing other than a (spiraling) return to very plausible or defensible etymologies: under this changed semantic regime, the antiracists would very logically be the dastardly enemies of races, those who hold that they do not exist, and who, in order to prove themselves right, work towards their disappearance, towards their fusion into a single race, in keeping with the wishes and interests of the industrialists and shareholders of Undifferentiated Human Matter (UHM); whereas the good racists, for their part, would after this revolution ("*Movement of an object that, observing a closed curve, etc...*")[7] be the friends of races, of all races without exception, seeing to their perpetuation and to the well-being of each of them, first and foremost the least numerous and most threatened among them.

Not surprisingly, it would be most difficult to win acceptance for this last point: that, despite its appalling connotations over the better part of the twentieth century, *racism* should be seen as a positive thing. In support of it, one might at least marshal the claim that it is consistent with ecology. And it is indeed odd that, fighting as hard as they can and ever-so legitimately for the maintenance or restoration of biodiversity in the world, the ecologists' demands seem to stop short at man, and to make an exception for him. Yet they should be the first to call themselves *racists*, in our inverted sense of the term, and pride themselves on it: not after the fashion of Houston Stewart Chamberlain, Alfred Rosenberg, or Vacher de Lapouge,[8] of course, but rather on the model of Montaigne, Malherbe (*What will you say, future races...*), Racine, Chateaubriand, Bernanos, General de Gaulle ("We are above all a European people of the white race, Greek and Latin culture... etc."), and Georges Pompidou—it is true that none of them ever dreamt (no more than I myself...) of assuming such an epithet, but then no one ever thought of forbidding them use of the word *race*.

The taboo on this term is relatively recent at the scale of human history, and, as we saw at the beginning, the event that triggered it was not, or at least not directly, the Second World War and its atrocities. It would doubtless be better to seek it instead (and more trivially) in the first or second oil crisis (1973 and 1979, respectively), family reunification (instituted by decree on April 29th, 1973), or the Yom Kippur War (6-24 October 1973). In an oft-quoted and remarked passage from my own *Journal*, I recounted a conversation I had with President Valéry Giscard d'Estaing at the Château de Varvasse, in Chanonat, on March 23rd, 2009, during which the former head of state rather curiously remarked: if "all these absurd laws" were passed, it was in short to appease the Jews of France, who under his presidency had become anxious, partly due to the recent influx of Jews from North Africa, who were "very different from the Jews more formerly observed on the territory and who did not always get along so well with them." It was also at this time, the former president continued, that "it began to be said, following Lévi-Strauss [I am certain of the reference to Lévi-Strauss, which came as a bit of a surprise in this context],[9] that there *are no races*, which is absurd, but they stuck to it, no doubt for fear of finding themselves isolated. Of course, there are races, as among fish [Pierre, to whom I reported these remarks, found that fish are not a very good analogy, that cats and dogs would have better fit the bill], but one must not say so: it's absurd, but in the end none of it really matters..."*

President Giscard d'Estaing seems very fond of the word *absurd*, which he pronounces through heavily pursed lips while blowing a little, like a little steam cooker.

A year and a half later, recounting a meeting with Alain Finkielkraut,[10] who found himself in the same hotel as I in Strasbourg, the following volume of the *Journal* revisits my conversation with Valéry Giscard d'Estaing in Chanonat:

> *"Thursday, September 23rd, 12:30 am.* Tuesday morning, had breakfast at the Strasbourg Sofitel with Finkielkraut, who was returning directly to Paris. I don't know how but the conversation turned—ah, yes, I was talking to him about the *2009 Journal*, the draft of which I am now revising and certain parts of which I would not be surprised to see censored...—to Valéry Giscard d'Estaing. I told him about the remarks the former president had made to me the year before, according to which the dogma of the non-existence of races had been proclaimed to make the Jews happy, as they were becoming anxious in the 1970s. According to Finkielkraut, the need to *make the Jews happy* was very present in Giscard's mind, for the same Giscard had told him, Finkielkraut, who was questioning him

---

*   *Krakmo, Journal 2009*, Fayard, pp. 175–176.

about family reunification, that this measure had been taken to *make Simone Veil happy...*[11]

"Whatever the case, few decisions have been of such historic moment..."*

The last sentence seems only to have related to family reunification but might just as well concern what the text calls, quite rightly in my opinion, the *dogma of the non-existence of races*. The manner in which this dogma was proclaimed was so severe, sudden, and solemn that it quickly came to constitute the better part of what was taught in school—a fact all the more noticeable as the heritage actually transmitted by way of education was then in the process of shrinking to next to nothing around it. If the school system could no longer teach more than one single subject, one single precept, it had to be this one. It preferred to abandon everything—literature, language, grammar, history, mathematics—rather than abandon it. Of course, having been only recently established, it had obviously never been part of any earlier intellectual or cultural heritage. And, indeed, it went against everything one had serenely thought for centuries. It nevertheless constituted the ultimate remnant, the final vestige, the impregnable foundation of transmission. If nothing else could be taught children, they would at least be taught this. All knowledge, all morality (and first and foremost civic morality) was summed up in this ideological *credo quia absurdum* (as Valéry Giscard d'Estaing would have put it), with the result that, if people only know one thing today (and it is not so unusual...), it is that there are no races. On this point, they are categorical. The more they know nothing, the more they know this.

The two decisions that the former president of the Republic mentioned to me—the proclamation of this dogma and that of family reunification—are closely contemporaneous. Both were

---

* *Parti Pris, Journal 2010*, Fayard, pp. 393–394.

products of the same ideological climate, of what one might call the *second antiracism*. The *first* antiracism, issuing directly from the death camps and the *never again!* to which their discovery gave rise, sought to defend races against one another, to protect the weakest against the strongest. The *second* antiracism, this one much more radical than the *first*, simultaneously posited, in a contradiction that continues to compromise its entire logical structure, that races are equal, which is not new, and that they do not exist, which is rather more so but which in these years would receive the confirmation of science, the only unquestioned authority in this era of all-out secularization, of the *scientization* of the experience of living.

That this authority should be unquestioned does not entirely imply that it is infallible, unquestionable. Contrary to what one might believe and that it would like one to believe, science is far from being independent of the political authorities, particularly the most powerful amongst them, ideological authority, the *dominant ideology* (that *pleonasm*, as Barthes called it)—let's call it *the spirit of the times*. Notwithstanding the counter-example of Galileo and a few others, which is moreover worth examining more closely, and which, given the opposing forces, does not necessarily mean what one takes it to mean, science has a marked tendency to only ever discover what its time, the spirit of its time (which is not necessarily embodied by the government, far from it…), wants it to discover, *needs* it to discover. This remark is all the truer, of course, for the aforementioned "human sciences" and the "soft" sciences in general than it is for the "hard" sciences—which, however, are not entirely shielded from all influence, which is sometimes insistent, indeed, all the more insistent in that it need not necessarily express itself in words, that it *is* the spirit of the times. Above all, science has a marked tendency to *not* discover anything that runs too directly counter to the sensibility of its era; or instead, if the discovery has unfortunately been made, to sweep it under the carpet.

To make myself understood, I will ask you to imagine what would happen to a young scholar should he today discover (*God forbid*—that's all we need!) that women's intellectual capacity is 17.48% lower than that of men. Does one believe that this scholar, no matter how rigorously he carried out his study, would be acclaimed for miles around by the academic and civil authorities? That peer-reviewed journals would fight over the honor of publishing the results of his research? That ministers of Research, Higher Education, and the Woman's Question would immediately open a line of credit for him to pursue the aforementioned research, offering him new laboratories and immediately providing him with a bevy of fully dedicated assistants? It is immensely more likely that our unfortunate scholar would there and then find himself obliged to give up all hope of ever having a career. Every era has a passionate hatred for bad ideological news—news that contradicts what it has decided is just and good to believe, news that seems to bely the precepts of what it conceives as the good. It does not consider truth to be an attribute of virtue (we are here still speaking of "ideological" virtue, of course), but virtue to be a major component of truth. In a general way, what is true in its eyes is what conforms to its *Weltanschauung*. Conversely, an allegation is not false because it does not have the facts on its side but rather because it is regarded as criminal or merely very unwelcome. Consider, for example, all that concerns the question of mean IQ: here one has a domain where science has for ages made precious few "discoveries." Have they been too scandalous, "unmanageable"? This prohibition appears to be lifting somewhat, perhaps for the simple reason that Westerners no longer achieve such good comparative results in this contest: if the tests can harm the privileged, humiliate the pride of the dominant or those reputed to be such, they are no longer so "morally" reprehensible.

For my part, I suspect that science has rarely shown itself so subservient, so eager to lend its support to the desiderata of power than it has with this recently proclaimed dogma, the non-existence of race. What it primarily has going against it, and that makes it a little suspicious, even in the eyes of an ignoramus like me, is how narrowly this universal dogma is applied, since it is almost only in France that races are so rigorously taboo, to such an extent that one seeks to eliminate any mention of them from the Constitution and laws. In the vast majority of other countries in the world, one seems to make do with them without too much trouble, as has been the case everywhere on Earth for forty centuries, for the better and, of course, for the worse.

It is my impression that, for any word, no matter how deeply embedded it might be in the language (and, indeed, the more deeply embedded, the easier it becomes, for there are then more angles of attack), one may always select or concoct a meaning so eccentric, so narrow and limited, that there is then nothing easier than to proclaim that what this vocable denotes does not exist. Indeed, it would be useful to draw up a list of the ideological authorities' favorite methods for discrediting their opponents, more precisely, their favorite methods for relieving them of their words, for preventing them from using these words on the grounds that they do not and cannot define them, that they are incapable of supplying a precise, "scientifically" and sometimes geographically unassailable definition of them, as in the case of *Europe*; but one might just as well cite *French*, or *people*, or *Muslim*, or *black*, etc.

Europe, on this view, thus has no meaning because it is impossible to fully reach agreement as to the precise boundaries of this continent. Similarly, French people do not exist, except perhaps on paper, because no one has ever been able to define them in a way that satisfies everyone and above all encompasses all aspects of the question or concept. One must not say "the Arabs" when speaking of Muslims because not all Arabs are Muslims. One must not say "Muslims" when speaking of Arabs, even in France, because not all Muslims are Arabs, far from it. This hackneyed and tiresome quibbling, which always takes the other for an imbecile, or an extremely ignorant person, or in bad faith, stems from a very profound misunderstanding as to the nature and purpose of definitions. It would be helpful to define the word *definition*. These methods for obstructing debate presuppose or pretend to presuppose that the definition precedes a word and even the thing it denotes; that the definition is a kind of fundamental law and first principle that unequivocally and once and for all posits what are words and what are things, which will then have to obediently conform to it or give up on being exchanged or even existing. But definition has never been that. With the possible exception of deliberate neologisms—*bathmology, genosuicide, faussel* (but if the neologism "takes," this exception does not last, and the new word begins to do whatever it likes...)[12]—the definition has never come first. It has never preceded what it defined. To the contrary, it has forever chased after words and things, trying to circumscribe them as well as it can, as precisely and narrowly as it is able. Yet it never entirely succeeds: if not, the map would be as large as the territory, the back cover as long as the novel, the story within the story indistinguishable from the narrative "frame" in which it is embedded. There is always some *play*, thank God: literature, for example, or style, or humor; and, even when they are crowned with success, the definition's efforts to exactly coincide with what it defines are forever threatened by challenges, misunderstandings, incidents along its borders.

The more difficult words are to define (*people, nation, race, culture, real*, etc.), the more the things they denote *are*. Recalcitrance vis-à-vis its definition, the stubborn tendency to everywhere spill its banks, but also, at times, to not fully occupy it, and of course to contradict it—for an object or concept, these are the signs par excellence of vitality. Against Wittgenstein, Gadamer; and against Hermogenes, Cratylus. To paraphrase and correct Voltaire— and to advance the conversation, to say nothing of "debates"—it is approximation, not knavery, that is the stock and trade of dictionaries.

Sometimes, and especially for the richest and most complex words, those most anciently and polysemously inscribed in the language—and the word *race* is eminently one of these—a single definition is not up to the job, several are needed: sometimes two or three, sometimes ten or twelve, sometimes even twenty. Yet if, late in the day, science was able to decide, in very authoritarian fashion, that races do not exist, it was because, immediately before doing so, it saw to it that race was conceived only in a very specific sense, one that was far from representative of the semantic range exhibited by this term. Apart from its narrowness, which is already regrettable in itself, this sense of the word has the very regrettable particularity of being, as I have already noted, the purely scientific or pseudo-scientific one in which racists (in the old sense, not in the one I offer…) understood it.

I am admittedly not competent to judge of the pertinence of the scientific reasoning or experimental demonstration that led to the peremptory conclusion that races do not exist. They always struck me as very uncertain, extremely unstable, changing according to the occasion and context. In the version given by Wikipedia, which is surely neither the best nor the worst source, they are presented as follows: "Since the mid-twentieth century, scientific studies based on genetics have shown that the concept of 'race' is not relevant in characterizing the various geographical subgroups of the human species because the genetic variation between individuals within a single population subgroup is greater than the average genetic variation between two different geographical subgroups."

Gosh… And further along: "Since the sequencing of the human genome was completed in 2004, some genetic analyses based on genetic polymorphisms have claimed that certain relevant polymorphisms of the human genome are distributed by 'geographical group' at sufficient allelic frequency. Although, as Professor Jens Reich notes, humans share 99.9% of their genes (or 99.5% according to the geneticist Craig Venter), as compared to humans and chimpanzees, which share 98.7%, Luigi Luca Cavalli-Sforza's team suggests that Homo Sapiens are distributed between nine 'base-populations,' while at the same time pointing out that, 'in reality, the idea of *race* serves no purpose for the human species. The structure of human populations is extremely complex; it varies from one region of the world to another, from one people to another; one always encounters an infinite number of gradations due to constant migration within borders and across borders, which makes neat distinctions impossible."

One must always be wary of people who say this or that *serves no purpose*: speak for yourself! Poetry also serves no purpose, nor do the white spaces of the menu on which all of our favorite dishes appear, between absence and uselessness. "God is a hypothesis of which I have no need," said Laplace to Napoleon, who quite rightfully mocked him. In passing, one will have spotted the hackneyed and always extremely effective argument known as *the argument from imprecise borders*, according to which things, concepts, categories do not exist because they interpenetrate one another, their borders are porous and fuzzy, it is impossible to rigorously separate them. With this way of reasoning, and above all of preventing others from reasoning, and of speaking (because that is what is at issue), it is easy to establish the non-existence of anything and everything: colors, civilizations, artistic schools and movements, peoples, historical phenomena. Who would dare claim the color red exists when it very imperceptibly verges on yellow, on the one hand, and blue, on the other, passing through orangeness on this flank, mauve and purple on the other? And the less said about black and white, the better. It is not entirely unthinkable (it would be a good selling point on his part) that tomorrow some historian will make a name for himself by claiming that the French Revolution never took place, that it is an outmoded notion, chock full of misunderstandings and intolerable ideological distortions: the revolution lasted nearly fifty years, and it was global, beginning with the American Revolution and ending somewhat pathetically with the Congress of Verona (let's say).

The vulgar version of the dogma of the non-existence of races seems unfathomably stupid but it is so often put forward, at least in an offhand way, that one cannot entirely ignore it here. It consists in saying that there are no races because all humans can reproduce among themselves, no matter the ethnic group to which they belong. To which the obvious response is that, in the animal kingdom, all sorts of races are perfectly interfertile, dogs being just the best known example: Labradors with Brittanies, poodles with Great Danes, setters with collies, and so on. The somewhat desperate objection to this objection, which is more than a little dangerous, even ideologically, is that man is not an animal, that the comparison is in bad taste, that it reduces the human being to the status of an animal, etc.—in insisting on this, one exposes oneself to the reproach of *speciesism*, a collection of opinions that are also not for their part especially well regarded these days, bestowing as they do a privileged position in nature upon the human species and conferring a right over animals that is contested by animal lovers.

The truth is that man has always been considered an animal, if not necessarily "like the others," and indeed it is to this fact that he owes the highest and most spiritual expressions of himself, the soul (*anima*). Men and mammals share an endless number of attributes—eyes, ears, teeth, heart, skin, respiration—and there is absolutely no reason why they should not also share the division of species into races. I am here employing the terminology of Linnaeus, which was legal tender for more than two centuries without incurring the least criticism: species and, within species, interfertile races. As the CNRS' André Pichot wrote in *Le Monde* on October 4th, 1996:

> In biology, race is a subdivision of species. It joins together individuals who, individual differences not-withstanding, all present some hereditary particular-ities that are sufficiently pronounced such that they may be clearly characterized as a group but not so pronounced that this group forms a distinct species.
>
> The definition is vague: the relevant character-istics are not specified, nor is the boundary beyond which their variation results in membership in one race rather than another. Due to their interfertility, moreover, there may be a regular gradation between the races thereby defined (the species is therefore always the basic taxonomical unit).
>
> It is nevertheless true that, for men and plants alike, different races exist, in all likelihood the prod-uct of geographical isolation and endogamy. It is fairly easy to distinguish between them, even if there is often little reason to do so, for their definition, impre-cise though it may be, is not totally arbitrary.[13]

Races are interfertile, species are not. As Robert Antelme aptly reminded us, it is of the *human species* that one speaks.[14]

One also says, albeit much less frequently, the *human race*, and in this respect it is unique. And why not, after all? For this is precisely what I am trying to establish or recall: that *race* is an immensely malleable word, one which, over the course of its long history, has meant almost everything and (nearly) its opposite. This is why it is absurd to go around repeating, in an ever-more threat-ening tone, in support of which appeal would soon be made to the 17th Chamber,[15] that what was never more than one of its meanings among dozens of others has no scientific relevance. Apart from the fact that, as I understand things, the matter has not been altogether settled—if it had been then why do some diseases only affect some ethnic groups and not others? why should some biological transfers be impossible between some specific portions of the human family? and why do the instructions accompanying certain medicines indicate that patients from this or that *race*—that is the word that is used—are at a higher risk than others for this or that side effect?—apart from the fact, then, that the matter has not been altogether settled, and even seems to be less and less so, in what way does this nullify a word upon which only racists and, alas, antiracists after them have claimed to confer scientific meaning?

To those who maintain, and almost everyone does, that the term "race" has no legitimacy in the scientific domain, where it is claimed there is no support for it, one might reply, at the price of a little imprecision, that one entirely shares their opinion. *Race* is not a scientific word; it is vastly more than that. Some have long sought and sometimes still seek to replace it with *ethnic group*, which straightaway has a whiff of the laboratory about it and which in their eyes has the advantage of not making such a poor impression, of not so flagrantly alerting the censor, of not causing you so much trouble. But to go along with this would be to consent to the most total misunderstanding. *Ethnic group* is to *race* what *homosexuality* is to the love of Achilles and Patroclus, David and Jonathan, Montaigne and Boetius—which were perhaps not cases of love (a question of definition, as with everything else) and therefore probably in no way scientific.

Do *family*, *people*, *nation* have any "scientific" meaning? And, should they not, will we be told that what these words designate *does not exist*? More than one are itching to do so, it is true, and some have already succumbed.

It is to be noted that each of the three terms I have just offered as examples has been, to varying degrees, synonymous with *race*.

Family is even the first meaning given by Littré: "all those who are of the same family."[16]

He quotes Mme de Sévigné on the Cardinal de Retz: "His entire race is clever, and he most of all" (18 September 1676).

The race in question is that of the Gondi.[17]

One could just as well here cite Montaigne, who laments that an over-reliance on estate names has obscured the transmission of patronyms and made it more difficult to make out lineages: "To conclude our account: it is a wicked custom and of very ill consequence for our France, to call each by the name of his land and seigneurie, and that thing in the world that most makes one confuse and mistake races." (*Essays*, I, XLVI)[18]

In *Phaedra*, neither Hippolyte nor Racine understood it any differently:

> *At the gates of Troezen,*
> *'Mid ancient tombs where princes of my race*
> *Lie buried, stands a temple, ne'er approach'd*
> *By perjurers*[19]

The most recent edition of the *Grand Larousse encyclopédique*[20] mentions the expression *to have something by race*, which it explains as follows: "To exhibit a characteristic that one owes to one's family origin." It offers this definition as (*lit.*).

In the sense of *family*, the word has taken on a somewhat specialized connotation, referring to the rather particular case of dynastic families. In France, it was once commonplace to hear talk of *kings of the first, second*, and *third race* (the Merovingians, Carolingians, and Capetians, respectively):

> "Towards the commencement of the first race, we meet with an infinite number of freemen" (Montesquieu, *Spirit of the Laws*, XXX, XI).

> "With the third race, the history of the Franks ends
> and that of the French begins" (Chateaubriand,
> *Analyse raisonnée de l'histoire de France*).[21]

Following the 1830 Revolution, the same Chateaubriand considered—or *pretended to consider*, for he on no account desired
this—the possibility of changing dynasty:

> Rejected after the July Days, the Republic raised the
> question of the total change of the Royal Race [...]
> Several argue that a revolution that has changed every-
> thing in a monarchic state only consolidates itself and
> comes to an end by a total change of Race. The people
> chose a new king, who had played no part in events; a
> king to whom the parties could make no reproach; a
> king who brings neither ties of kinship, nor prejudice,
> nor grudge to the throne; a king who has nothing to
> reward, nothing to avenge, who no ruination inflames
> or indicts [...] All is thus clear in the choice of a new
> Race; it is, as in the case of a Republic, a comprehensive
> measure [...] The Republic having been ruled out, a
> new Race not promoted to the crown, there remained
> the choice between two legitimacies: the Duke of
> Bordeaux, heir of a great race; the Duke of Reichstadt,
> heir of a great man ("On the New Proposal Relating to
> the Banishment of Charles X and His Family").

Going back over a thousand years, the partial but very extensive coincidence between the meanings of *race* and those of *family*
or *dynasty* allows one to better grasp the chronological coincidence
(sometime around the mid-nineteen seventies of the twentieth
century) between what I have moreover, *very* moreover, called the
Little Replacement and the Great: to wit, the change of culture and

the change of people; the change of class and the change of race. From the point of view of cultural and economic privileges, as from the allied point of view of political power, the social hierarchy of races, as long as they existed, was an almost exact counterpart of the social hierarchy of classes. There was an almost perfect homomorphism between the conditions and degree of comfort of each. By virtue of their advantages and the power they had acquired for themselves, whites were for several centuries the aristocracy and then the bourgeoisie of the world, as well as of the various countries in which they shared or share the territory with non-whites, or with those whom the most recent development of actually existing language curiously calls *racialized people*, as if the privilege of being a race or belonging to a race should be reserved for them (and be refused to whites). And indeed, by virtue of the position they long enjoyed in the hierarchy of acquired or imposed advantages, whites invited resentment at least as keen as that felt, in the hierarchy of class positions, by the proletariat or petty bourgeoisie for the old dominant classes: a form of resentment so well captured by Nietzsche and that we today see so clearly at work, vengeful and destructive, in conjunction with the "Little Replacement." If whites were the aristocracy of the world, we are now in 1793; and if they were its bourgeoisie, we are now in 1936 or 1968.

But let's instead return to 1975, the year "one middle school"[22] was established in France and the approximate moment that the dogma of the non-existence of races, to stick with my terminology, was proclaimed. The establishment of "one middle school" was probably the most palpable blow ever struck against the old bourgeois culture, against the bourgeois conception of culture, and was to render it indefensible in both senses of the word: impossible to protect, to sustain, and impossible to praise, to extol, to laud. Those who might seek to oppose the Little Replacement would be exposed to that absolute weapon of language, the accusation of *class contempt*, or snobbery; just as those who might seek to oppose the Great would run the unbearable risk of that other, yet more fearsome and destructive accusation, that of *race contempt*, or racism.

It was roughly at this time, 1975, that culture no doubt irreversibly transitioned (a transition admirably reflected, from one day and hour to the next, on radio stations such as France Culture)[23] from culture as patrimony, heritage, the voice of the dead to culture as leisure activity, entertainment, hobby, a way of passing the time, a way of killing it. The change of language, in the meaning of words, in the class of reference that this involved for culture is precisely that which the present work seeks to account for, for they are one and the same.*

The central figure here is obviously Pierre Bourdieu. The phenomenon certainly would have taken place without him, all the more so as it is a global development. Nevertheless, Bourdieu was one of its essential tools, if not its main one, notably in his role as logothete—he who assigns names, words, language—for this shift from the vertical to the horizontal in culture, particularly as it relates to time: from a society of heirs, such as he denounces, to a society of *non-heirs*, as I believe I was the first to call them, in reference to him of course; from social reproduction to the eternal *da capo*, the constant return to the point of departure.

The symbolic abolition of races merely extended the same phenomenon—the temporal shift from the vertical to the horizontal in what concerns people—to the entire planet. In keeping with the demand for equality, they, too, must have no ancestors, no inheritance, no atavism, no race. What they are only depends on them, from one day to the next. As for culture and the educational system, this, too, is the eternal *da capo*, the fantasy of self-creation for societies and nations, as for men. The proclamation of the dogma of the non-existence of races, which makes it impossible to defend peoples

---

* *Dictionnaire des délicatesses du français contemporain, op. cit.*

against the immigrant floodtide, is precisely contemporaneous with the establishment of "one middle school," which makes it impossible to defend culture against the floodtide of so-called "culturally disadvantaged" classes (all the more so as the most disadvantaged of these classes are obviously comprised of immigrants).

Forty centuries believed in the mildness and virtue of *age-old roots*, as the poet says.[24] Social inequality was essentially based on whether or not one belonged to a *good family*, that is, an old, long-established family, one that therefore had something precious to pass on in what concerned the experience of the world and knowledge (including, of course, knowledge of *social relations*).

In the name of equality, modernity or its sequel have fiercely broken with this classic, but universal and age-old, arrangement. Indeed, to paraphrase the contemporary way of speaking and the tics of historians, one might speak of the *invention of the present*. Following Casimir Brandys and Danièle Sallenave,* I have long pointed out that the ignorance of history, which clearly keeps growing, no longer consists in not knowing what may have happened in the sixteenth or seventeenth centuries, but in not knowing that there are centuries at all, in not understanding this concept, nor even that of the past itself. The man of the two Replacements, the replaceable man, is the man without memory, without vertical family, without lineage, without race, without culture, without history. His memory has been given over to computers and specialists, who do with it what they will. He is condemned to the present and, like it, indefinitely replaceable, replaced from birth.

In this context, the hereditary monarchies, the dynasties, the kingly, imperial, or princely races that kept their thrones despite the revolutions of the twentieth century appear as karstic reliefs, outcroppings of great symbolic interest, but whose positions will become harder and harder to maintain, since everything

---

*   Sallenave, Danièle, *Le Don des morts*, Gallimard, 1991.

legitimating them has now collapsed around them (with the possible exception of Japan?). How can they carry on alone on the strength of hereditary, inherited rights in the midst of a world that has abolished these things all around, starting with those of the nobility? If nothing is to be inherited, neither peerages, nor culture, nor manners, nor civilization, nor even family homes (this is being seen to now), how long can the crown itself hold out?

It is clear that, if they are to survive, monarchies must hastily see to it that they become social and racial commoners: in what concerns privileges, whether they be economic or cultural, the social hierarchy of races, as we have remarked or suggested, was the exact counterpart of the social hierarchy of classes. For kings, it is a matter of dispensing with their ancestors as quickly as possible, of exiting their lineages, of forsaking the verticality of races. And yet they owe everything to them. What to do?

Here as elsewhere, the marvelous plasticity of the concept and word *race* should offer a way out thanks to its antiquity and immense semantic wealth, which the stupid racists wished to stupidly reduce to just one thing, under cover of science or pseudo-science. The families and dynasties referred to by the word race can very well be families of spirit, of mores, of habits, of strengths or weaknesses—the *race of poets*, the *race of amateur painters*, the *miserly race*, the *race of heroes*, the *race of the Nimrods* (Balzac)—and, in this sense, though perhaps eternal, can be more horizontal than vertical, less linked to inheritance than to simultaneous similarity of condition, hobby, character, temperament:

> "There exist two races, the selfish race of pure interest, and the sympathetic race of duty and law" (Lamennais, preface to *De l'esclavage modern*).

> "Unknown to him, whether he wishes it or not, whether he consents to it or not, the author of this

immense and strange work is of the strong race of rev-
olutionary writers. Balzac gets straight to the point"
(Hugo on Balzac, at the latter's funeral).

"The race of gladiators is not dead, every artist is one.
He amuses the public with his agonies" (Flaubert, letter to Ernest Feydeau).

"She and I deny what we are supposed to be," says *The
Cardinal of Spain* of Mad Queen Joan. "We do not
belong to the same race. Those who have looked upon
what she calls nothing and I call God have the same
eyes" (Montherlant).

One might continue in this way without end. For Proust, it
is homosexuals who are a race, supplying zealous contemporary
commentators with grist for their mill to attack him on two fronts:

I now understood, moreover, how, earlier in the day,
when I had seen him coming away from Mme. De
Villeparisis', I had managed to arrive at the conclusion that M. de Charlus looked like a woman: he was
one! He belonged to that race of beings, less para-
doxical than they appear, whose ideal is manly simply because their temperament is feminine and who
in their life resemble in appearance only the rest of
men; there where each of us carries, inscribed in those
eyes through which he beholds everything in the universe, a human outline engraved on the surface of the
pupil, for them it is that not of a nymph but of a youth.
Race upon which a curse weighs and which must live
amid falsehood and perjury, because it knows the
world to regard as a punishable and a scandalous, as

an inadmissible thing, its desire; which must deny its God, since even Christians, when at the bar of justice they appear and are arraigned, must before Christ and in His Name defend themselves, as from a calumny, from the charge of what to them is life itself; sons without a mother, to whom they are obliged to lie all her life long and even in the hour when they close her dying eyes; friends without friendships, despite all those which their charm, frequently recognized, inspires and their hearts, often generous, would gladly feel; but can we describe as friendship those relations which flourish only by virtue of a lie and from which the first outburst of confidence and sincerity in which they might be tempted to indulge would make them be expelled with disgust, unless they are dealing with an impartial, that is to say sympathetic mind, which however in that case, misled with regard to them by a conventional psychology, will suppose to spring from the vice confessed the very affection that is most alien to it, just as certain judges assume and are more inclined to pardon murder in inverts and treason in Jews for reasons derived from original sin and racial predestination. (*Sodom and Gomorrah*)[25]

With the end of this quotation, we return to a narrower, more familiar, and more contemporary meaning of the word *race*, which alas is to say more "problematic"; and it is here all the more "problematic" as it concerns the Jewish "race," which, for eminently comprehensible reasons, is particularly keen to not exist, or at least to not be referred to in this manner, not by others in any case. It was more or less in this way that the disastrous "Camus Affair" began in 2000. The journalist Marc Weinstein,[26] commissioned, I believe, by *Les Inrockuptibles*, wished to hear from my mouth confirmation that I had indeed mentioned the "Jewish race" in my *Journal* for the year 1994, *La Campagne de France*. I think that, six years later, I hardly recalled having done so, but it did not in the least strike me as impossible. Above all, I did not see the point of the question. Oh dear, must one not speak of the *Jewish race*? Doubtlessly not, but, in the twenty or twenty-five years that this unwritten rule had (as far as I know) existed, I had not had the time to take cognizance of it. As I took little interest in these ideological questions at the time, I had not seen this shift in the wind. It was in all innocence that I said *race*, whether it be for natives of the Auvergne like myself, spendthrifts, or hypochondriacs, in the same way that I said *nègre* or *Mademoiselle*,[27] may God forgive me. My vocabulary did not begin in 1975 (it is rather there that it ended). And I have difficulty seeing why something that was so innocent for five or six centuries should become criminal from one day to the next; and that, what is worse, it should become so as a result of cultural and social developments that do not appear to me to demand immediate and unanimous admiration, for neither the soul, nor the spirit, nor the dignity of existence has gained anything from them, no more than has the beauty of the world.

In what concerns the *Jewish race*, I could have taken shelter behind illustrious examples, among them Jews. Léon Blum, for instance, frequently talked of *his race*. And do not say that this was before the concentration camps, which supposedly changed everything; it was right in their sinister midst. As Blum wrote from Buchenwald on July 31st, 1944: "But what may be of interest, what will even have an influence on some of my friends in F. and elsewhere, is that, in writing here, from the depths of my prison in Ger., in the midst of the boundless horrors from which my country, my party, my race all suffer, I so faithfully repeat what I have said and written elsewhere, in other times."*

---

*   *Lettres de Buchenwald*, edited with a preface by Laurent Greisammer, Gallimard, "Témoins" collection, 2003, p. 143.

In short, until the generation before last, it might be said that there was not a single French writer, poet, philosopher, intellectual, orator, or politician who did not make use of the word *race*, in all of its conceivable meanings, most of which were entirely peaceful. And then all of a sudden, for not terribly convincing, indeed rather suspicious, scientific reasons, which in any case only took account of a very narrow segment of its meaning, and not the most interesting one, it was said that one must do without it, if only from opportunism and deference? This prohibition is of the same kind as that forbidding or discouraging use of *Miss*, of the circumflex over *abîme*, and of the past preterit, also judged too discriminating.[28]

The paradox is that, since the abolition of race, the word and the thing, the word *because* of the thing, never has the thing been so spoken of, nor above all has its elusive, poorly circumscribed, but obstinate reality so vibrated within men's chests. That which holds for the evolution of races among us—their *post-mortem* evolution, that is, since it appears they no longer exist—is oddly reminiscent of what is frequently said of borders: that the more they are abolished *in toto*, the more they proliferate in detail. The more that countries are open, the more that houses are closed, locked, padlocked, indefinitely protected by countless metal gates and digital codes, which make social relations and getting around ever-more difficult, all the more so as mistrust prevails and that, in order to protect themselves in a world without external protection, both the authorities and individuals are driven to everywhere erect barriers, metal detectors, bollards, and to hire more security guards. Similarly, never have men and women so happily sung in their genealogical tree, so mechanically expressed their origins and belongings in their sentences, in their opinions, in their gestures, and in their stances; in short, never has race spoken through them more than since race ceased to exist. It has come to the point that it quite often, too often, suffices to know their name to know what they are going to say; to see their face to get a rather good, too good, idea of what they think (about the Israeli-Palestinian conflict, for example). The most accurate and, alas, also most proven model of our everyday hermeneutic is the prejudice of the trial lawyer as he goes about deciding whether to retain or dismiss a member of the jury on the basis of rather crude clues.

For better and for worse, it appears that the twenty-first century will be *racial* more than it will be social, sexual, or religious. To seek to prevent it from being so by striking words from the dictionary and from basic texts amounts to magical thinking—not science, and still less law. It is a whim of arrested development, of the spoiled manchild.

***

In the first part of his introduction to the *History of the French Revolution*, Michelet writes: "In her turn, the Revolution, the daughter of Christianity, has taught its lessons to the whole world, to every race, and to every religion under the sun."[29]

In a panic, the Pléiade edition thought it necessary to immediately add by way of note: "The word 'race' is here to be taken in its cultural-historical sense, with a pronounced national connotation—Augustin Thierry (1795–1856), for example, contrasts the Germanic 'race' with the Gallic 'race.'"

In short, yes, these authors speak French: the French that held sway until the last quarter of the twentieth-century. The specialized scientific or pseudo-scientific meaning that this note would deter one from taking into account in Michelet's sentence (quite rightly so, of course) is that of the racists, in the sense of this term that one would today be well-advised to move beyond: it is thus immensely regrettable that this "racist" meaning of the word race should be the one adopted by antiracism and antiracists, both as the latter term is commonly understood (the defenders of threatened races) and in the new meaning that I propose for it (those who deny the concept of race and the existence of all races).

***

"But we have a more pressing reason to approve of these revelations, despite the additional worry they inflict upon us: French opinion must take the measure of the blow that has been dealt our race [...] In truth, this is the only problem, the one upon which the solution to all others depends, for if we save the race, the rest will be given us in surplus."

And a little later: "To be sure, in what concerns France, it is not enough to say that nothing is lost and all can still be saved: [...] the first of our duties, and it can even be said our only duty, since it sums up all the others: to save the race" (François Mauriac, *Journal, Mémoires politiques*, April 1945, Robert Laffont, 2008).

Having quoted these few sentences, I received a torrent of abuse from a woman presenting herself as one of Mauriac's relatives and who gave me to understand in no uncertain terms that the word *race* as he used it there in no way had the meaning that I gave it. But precisely the opposite is true: the word *race* as he used it has precisely (which is to say, *imprecisely*) the meaning I wished it to have; and not at all the very limited and "precise" one (scientifically "precise," that is) that the old racists and new antiracists have unanimously given it.

The Deep Murmur

I see that this short speech* received a title before its first word was even written: "*Ethnos* and *Polis*." These are two, immensely rich concepts, which might supply the object of fascinating discussions. They gave rise to an erudite little book by Henri Levavasseur, *L'Identité, socle de la cité*, the subtitle of which, as it happens, is *Réconcilier ethnos et polis*.[1] They have only one drawback in my eyes: they are not mine, I have never used them, a hundred authors and orators could discuss them before you better than I could. I prefer to stick to a single term that I believe essential and that I discussed at some length in a little book that is itself only an extract from a long entry in my *Dictionnaire des délicatesses du français contemporain*.[2] It is a term to make one tremble, it is true, even in this gathering. It is the word *race*.

Two preliminary considerations are in order, if you will. Writers are neither philosophers, nor intellectuals. They are the adherents of a mode of exploring and representing reality that was long the *French* mode par excellence, but which is now so little so that it is commonplace to hear our society described as *post-literary*, and to such an extent that the very nature of this way of apprehending the world is today no longer understood. Let us venture to define

---

* Speech delivered April 2nd, 2022, before the Institut Illiade colloquium, "Restaurer la politique: identité, souveraineté, sacré," held in Paris at the maison de la Chimie.

it, if you will, as the non-coincidence of meaning with itself, of words with their significations. And let us define literature, just this once, and in keeping with an old formula of mine, as "the indivisible remainder of the accounting operations of the real": one may make all the calculations one likes, one can thoroughly draw upon all the so-called human sciences, this is what resists, this indestructible monad—letters, poetry, novels, the sentence. I believe that the writer's mission is to systematically go to meet the blind spots of his society and of all societies, their no man's land, their forbidden zone, their Bermuda triangle, their Transylvanian mountains: there where every traveler loses his way, where he is lost before he even sets out. *Race* is one of these *loci desperati* of thought, its Carpathian castle, its Sargasso Sea. Many heroes have risked it, many vessels have ventured there, most never returned, or in what a state!

Second, and this will appear unrelated to my *first*, anyone or anything—a dragon, a storm god, a man, a group of men, a coalition of interests, or a machine, *several* machines, a *machination*—anyone or anything, I was saying, who intends to commit an appalling crime and escape all reproach, better yet be above all reproach, that person or that machine, that room of machines, that machination must have at their disposal what I have called *an absolute weapon of language*: a fearsome device for imposing silence, a nuclear shield, a Medusa-headed escutcheon that paralyses all opposition. For the Genocidal-Negationist Bloc, that which promotes the Great Replacement even as it denies that it is taking place, the word *race* ideally fills this role. The term is damned. Whoever uses it is a dead man. Indeed, it is a dead man who speaks to you now.

Yet it is essential to note that this curse is of recent date, entirely modern. It is not even fifty years old. General de Gaulle did not hesitate to speak of race and races, in sentences some of which are famous. One thinks of one in particular, quoted and requoted, about the French, who are above all a European people of white race, Greek and Latin culture, and Christian religion—all of you know it by heart.[3] Georges Pompidou spoke frequently about race, of the qualities and shortcomings *of our race*, and in what serve as his memoirs assured his readers that his parents were *of good French race*—a turn of phrase he gave an essentially *moral* sense, moreover, and in passing it cannot be overstated that the sole fact of speaking of the *French race* should suffice to prove that one is not *racist* in the antiracist sense of the term, the French race, like that of the atrabilious or readers of Montaigne, having very little in the way of an ethnic character.

What happened? What brought about the revolution and led to the curse, Georges Pompidou hardly in his grave?

The Great Replacement, or change of people and of civilization, or, to borrow an expression coined by Aimé Césaire, *the genocide by substitution*, is the crime against humanity of the twenty-first century. To observe its reality and put a name on it is in no way a *theory*, and even less a conspiracy theory. It is to offer a chrononym, a name for an era, our own, on the basis of its most striking phenomenon: one says *the Great Replacement* like one said *the Great Plague, the Great Schism, the Great Disturbance, the Great War*, or *the Great Depression*. To wish to believe or have others believe that phenomena of this scale might be the result of a *conspiracy* is to imagine that the French Revolution was an episode in the Affair of the Diamond Necklace and the Russian Revolutions the result of the rotten meat served the sailors of the Battleship Potemkin. It is to pay no heed to the comparative magnitude of cause and effect. If the Great Replacement is a conspiracy, and its denunciation a conspiracy theory, then all political aspirations and all economic and ideological forces at work throughout the world are conspiracies. Communism is a conspiracy, Nazism was a conspiracy, liberalism and ultra-liberalism are conspiracies par excellence—this is obviously absurd.

But the fact that phenomena are not conspiracies does not mean they are not crimes, that is, that there is not a will at work behind the scenes, the will of men, of groups of men, of nations, of social and economic forces, of financial mechanisms, of machines, and of machination. The Great Replacement is not a conspiracy; it is a machination, in the most comprehensive sense of the term, the transformation of man into machine, at once producer, consumer, and product.

What I called *davocracy*, the management of the human park by the great financiers, the banks, the pension funds, the multinationals, and the GAFAM empire, has two demands, each as contrary to any concern for ecology as the other: on the one hand, demographic growth, which, from the point of view of Davos, is nothing other than an indefinitely growing mass of consumers, this perpetual dodge or Ponzi scheme on which the maintenance of the economic bubble depends; on the other hand, the general interchangeability of the consumer-product *man*, that is, the fanatical reduction of human biodiversity. Yet to respond to the first of these demands, demographic growth, by means of the second, the elimination of biodiversity, davocracy sees to the systematic replacement of populations with low demographic growth rates by populations with high demographic growth rates. This replacement, which I repeat is the crime against humanity of the twenty-first century, since it is wiping out several of the highest civilizations on Earth before our eyes, is only possible on one condition: that it can be denied and repudiated, that there are no words to speak of it, that it be made inconceivable and unmentionable even as it is being carried out. For that, it is necessary that there be no fundamental difference, officially, between what is doing the replacing and what is being replaced; that this difference, if it exists, may not be named. And it is not the values of the Right, eminently differentialist as they are, that will ensure this abolition of difference for the industries of man, those that produce UHM, Undifferentiated

Human Matter; it is the values of the Left and, in particular, its two most precious and most honored ones—to wit, equality and antiracism, which is never anything but equality transposed from classes to races, just as secularism is never anything but equality transposed from the profane world to the world of religion.

I just said *races*, but this is of course what one must above all *not* say. For twenty or thirty centuries, the word *race* was spoken in all innocence, our literature and our poetry are replete with this vocable, in all its tremendous semantic complexity—*dynasty, lineage, elegance, chic, dog, branch, species, community*. But from one day to the next it was prohibited, on the grounds that it had no meaning, whereas the truth, as we have just seen, is that it has a hundred. The prohibition took the solemn form of the proclamation of the non-existence of races, the exact date of which, down to the very day, I cannot give, but which occurred around the middle of the nineteen-seventies of the twentieth century, at roughly the same time as the law on family reunification, which in France ushered in the Great Replacement, or genocide by substitution, and the Haby Law, which proclaimed the "one middle school" system, which is to say, for all intents and purposes, the suppression of social classes in education, or Little Replacement, with results that are only all too familiar.[4]

The dogma of the non-existence of races is of course in many respects bound up with the collapse of the educational system, but this is also because that dogma is nearly all that remains of it. When our contemporaries only know one thing, and this is increasingly common, above all among the youngest cohort, it is that there are no races. The system successively abandoned the teaching of every subject—literature, history, mathematics, grammar, spelling—but it was decided that one lesson would still be instilled in them, no matter the cost, and upon the ruins of all the others, and it was this: that there are no races. It is the smallest common denominator of knowledge. It is all that one knows when one knows nothing. That it is untrue only makes it all the more regrettable.

Whether it is false *scientifically*, I would not hazard to judge. I do not doubt that it is possible to adopt with regards to race such a deformed point of view that one subsequently has no trouble establishing, if such is the definition accepted, that races do not exist. Indeed, the affirmation that things *do not exist*, above all things whose disappearance it is actively bringing about, is the guilty pleasure of global replacism, of which antiracism is the faithful tool. Not only does everything it abolishes *not exist*, but it *has never existed*. French culture does not exist, the native French do not exist, France has always been a country of immigration, races never existed. We are here dealing with the first ever case of *retrospective* genocidal-negationism. All of the conditions for the perfect crime have come together. How can there be a genocide of peoples who do not exist, of races that, by definition, never existed? Even the Nazis, though they are in many respects the main inspiration for davocratic global replacism, the inventors and first practitioners of the Great Replacement, or *Umvolkung* in their parlance, even the Nazis did not go so far as to claim that the Jews had never existed.

Races took the news of their non-existence very badly, all the more so as no one has had the courtesy of informing them. Never in the course of world affairs or the formation of opinions have they weighed so heavily or shown themselves so quarrelsome, indeed throat-slashing, as they have since they no longer existed.

One anomaly of the dogma of the non-existence of races, which in truth is all anomaly, improbability, unbelievable approximation, is that it is completely untenable except on condition that the antiracists, its authors and promoters, take the word *race* in exactly the same sense as do the worst racists: that is, as a scientific or pseudo-scientific term. I am not too clear on what the scientific meaning of race is, that which caused, probably not without reason, its non-existence. Perhaps races do not exist according to science, though once again I have growing doubts on this score. I do not rule out, though again I hardly believe, the possibility that the Dogma's promoters might be great biologists. I am, by contrast, certain that they are dreadful linguists and semiologists. Yet linguistics and semiology are also officially considered to be sciences. And for them to claim that races do not exist would be just as absurd as to maintain that social classes do not exist, or the French, or the sexes. Once again, to maintain such a thing, it is necessary that the word be reduced to scarcely a twentieth part—the scientific or pseudo-scientific part—of the vast arc of its meanings; and this twentieth part, I repeat, was only of interest to strictly observant racists and, after them, the antiracists who made it their own without the least modification, if only to negate it in keeping with their wont.

The word *antiracism* has completely changed meaning, so much so that one might distinguish between two, completely different senses of the term: before and after the great reversal of the mid-nineteen-seventies, before and after the proclamation of the Dogma. The first antiracism was born of the ever-so legitimate *never again* of the death camps, which put it beyond all reproach; and to be sure there was nothing to reproach it for so long as it was protection from persecution of certain, particularly threatened races—Jews, blacks, gypsies, American Indians, and so on. The second antiracism, for its part, is the negation of the existence of races, it is the Dogma, it is so-called multiculturalism, this mass deculturation: the colonization of Europe, the genocide by substitution, the non-stop promotion of diversity and the change of people. Nothing would be more logical nor, in my view, more desirable than to symmetrically invert the word *racism*, which from that moment on would only mean the love of races, the belief in their existence, the organization of their peaceful coexistence, one and all. Consider this chiasmus: since it is antiracism that is now genocidal, if only by substitution, it is up to racism to see to the protection of men, women, races, peoples, animals, landscapes, and the Earth itself.

To be comfortable calling oneself a *racist* in this new and inverted sense, but one that is nevertheless more in keeping with its etymology and more logical than the received contemporary sense, would certainly take great courage. And, indeed, this heroism would have to be all the greater given that the Genocidal-Negationist Bloc, replacist davocracy and its henchmen, its journalists, its judges, its stalkers, its trolls, its dispensaries of denunciation, and its militias, which are legion, would be only too delighted to ignore the inversion, to pretend to not understand it, and to call into question its sincerity. But the profit would be great, I think. For it is here, on the subject of race, that we are each time held at bay and rendered totally incapable of expressing the simplest and truest things. It is because the genocidaires *control* race and know that it is a deadly weapon they hold in their hands that they give themselves over with such impunity to these endless games of cat and mouse where the unfortunates who resist the genocide by substitution are forced to beat a retreat whenever they are asked (on the model of the famous bearded Islamist, "And what allows you to think that I am a man?") what *exactly* gives them to believe that a car of the RER, or a neighborhood in Marseille, or yet another throat slit proves that the adherents of the Great Replacement are right. *What makes you think that? On what basis do you make this observation?* Without recourse to race, to its forbidden self-evidence, no reply is possible. And just like that the question is mainly settled in the eyes of the mainstream media—sorry, the *sewage stream*, genocidal negationist media.[5] It is taken for a fact that races do not exist, and one may now move on to other things, always with the aim of hewing to the desiderata of the industries of man, that of crushing the species, of hastening the universal advent of UHM. It is now the turn of the sexes, an easy target in the era of deconstruction, to learn that they do not exist, that they have never existed, that they are a social construction.

Race, the question of race, is the ratchet by means of which the replacist power keeps us in its grip. Caught in its deadly gears, we can neither retreat nor advance, no one being keen to call themselves *racist* in the absurd sense that traditional racists and antiracists of all stripes have agreed to give this word. Because of this, the sadistic cat can thus ask, for example: "I might be able to understand were you were to object to the supposed Islamization of society, but how can you have a problem with a fully integrated black Christian?" And to be sure, I have absolutely no problem with a fully integrated black Christian or, for that matter, *non-Christian*. France has always done a wonderful job integrating individuals from other civilizations, other peoples, and other races. She has given them much; they have given her much. But France absolutely cannot integrate tens of millions of blacks, or Asians, or Arabs, Christian or not Christian, fully integrated or not fully integrated. If only our dear antiracists would carry their reasoning through to its conclusion, its genocidal import would immediately become apparent. Not only would a France or a Europe in which sixty or seventy percent of its population was black, Arab, Korean, or American Indian obviously no longer be France, no longer be Europe, but it would still be necessary to answer to God and to man for the obliteration this would involve of their cultures and their indigenous populations.

For whomsoever would save the diversity of the world, its biodiversity, of which it will be agreed its ethnodiversity is an essential part, there is no way to forgo race and thus no alternative, in the eyes of antiracists, who have logically enough become its harshest critics, but to acknowledge oneself *racist* in the new sense noted above: that is, a champion of races and of their conservation, one and all.

I will refrain from offering the least definition of race, convinced as I am that the more things *are*—and race most certainly *is*—the less they are circumscribed by their definition. One would need at least twenty. With all due apologies to my regular customers, I prefer to once again fall back upon this sentence from Bernanos, which I consider to be one of the most beautiful in our language, and which is certainly not a definition, but which is far more eloquent for being suggestive: "Alas, around the little French boys huddled together over their notebooks, pen in hand, attentive and sticking out their tongues a little, like around young people drunk from their first outing beneath the flowering chestnut trees, in the arms of a young blonde girl, there was in times past that vague and enchanted memory, that dream, that deep murmur in which the race cradles its own."

A *deep murmur*, that, essentially, is what race is. Originating in the depths of time, in other words, it is, if not hereditary, then at least an inheritance. This is what cannot be forgiven it by the davocratic industries of man, which want a liquified humanity for the shanties of the global shantytown, without lumps, interchangeable at will, and which in inheritance only see inequality, which it undoubtedly is. Whence their horror of transmission, whether it be *cultural*, as in cultural literacy, respecting the authority of teachers, the education of attention (and this is why education and culture must be destroyed), or *material*, family homes, furniture, libraries, paintings (and this is why it is necessary to bedevil the patrimony, as well as patronyms and all that concerns fathers). Global replacism is a universal coalition against time. It wants a perpetual present of stupefaction, a continuous *da capo*, an incessant *great reset*. This is shown, among a thousand other examples, by the successive disappearance of moods and tenses (the future, future perfect, past preterit, imperfect subjunctive) from grammatical usage; the general substitution of given names for surnames, for *family* names, the sole testament of lineage; the de-historicization of everything, and first and foremost of space, with these nonsensical new regions, *Auvergne-Rhône-Alpes, PACA, Grand-Est, Hauts-de-France*,[6] and these agglomerations of towns bearing the names of shopping centers, housing estates, or retirement homes.

The *ethnos* is stretched to the breaking point. The presidential election is its last chance to reclaim its rights. Tomorrow, it will be done for, as will its millennial coincidence with the *polis*. The presidential election is in fact a referendum. There are twelve candidates, to be sure, but it is Eleven against one: on the one hand, the enthusiastic or resigned supporters of the status quo or its exacerbation, of the change of people and of culture, the change of race and of civilization, and, on the other, the sole candidate who rejects it and openly talks of turning back the Great Replacement, going so far as to invoke remigration. Between Éric Zemmour and the Eleven, I do not think I need to say how I will choose.

Appendix

Reproduced below is the full text of what has come to be known as Enoch Powell's "Rivers of Blood" speech, delivered to the Conservative Political Center in Birmingham, England, on April 20th, 1968:

> The supreme function of statesmanship is to provide against preventable evils. In seeking to do so, it encounters obstacles which are deeply rooted in human nature.
>
> One is that by the very order of things such evils are not demonstrable until they have occurred: at each stage in their onset there is room for doubt and for dispute whether they be real or imaginary. By the same token, they attract little attention in comparison with current troubles, which are both indisputable and pressing: whence the besetting temptation of all politics to concern itself with the immediate present at the expense of the future.
>
> Above all, people are disposed to mistake predicting troubles for causing troubles and even for desiring troubles: "If only," they love to think, "if only people wouldn't talk about it, it probably wouldn't happen."

Perhaps this habit goes back to the primitive belief that the word and the thing, the name and the object, are identical.

At all events, the discussion of future grave but, with effort now, avoidable evils is the most unpopular and at the same time the most necessary occupation for the politician. Those who knowingly shirk it deserve, and not infrequently receive, the curses of those who come after.

A week or two ago I fell into conversation with a constituent, a middle aged, quite ordinary working man employed in one of our nationalized industries.

After a sentence or two about the weather, he suddenly said: "If I had the money to go, I wouldn't stay in this country." I made some deprecatory reply to the effect that even this government wouldn't last forever; but he took no notice, and continued: "I have three children, all of them been through grammar school and two of them married now, with family. I shan't be satisfied till I have seen them all settled overseas. In this country in 15 or 20 years' time the black man will have the whip hand over the white man."

I can already hear the chorus of execration. How dare I say such a horrible thing? How dare I stir up trouble and inflame feelings by repeating such a conversation?

The answer is that I do not have the right not to do so. Here is a decent, ordinary fellow Englishman, who in broad daylight in my own town says to me, his Member of Parliament, that his country will not be worth living in for his children.

I simply do not have the right to shrug my shoulders and think about something else. What he is saying, thousands and hundreds of thousands are saying and thinking—not throughout Great Britain, perhaps, but in the areas that are already undergoing the total transformation to which there is no parallel in a thousand years of English history.

In 15 or 20 years, on present trends, there will be in this country three and a half million Commonwealth immigrants and their descendants. That is not my figure. That is the official figure given to parliament by the spokesman of the Registrar General's Office.

There is no comparable official figure for the year 2000, but it must be in the region of five to seven million, approximately one-tenth of the whole population, and approaching that of Greater London. Of course, it will not be evenly distributed from Margate to Aberystwyth and from Penzance to Aberdeen. Whole areas, towns, and parts of towns across England will be occupied by sections of the immigrant and immigrant-descended population.

As time goes on, the proportion of this total who are immigrant descendants, those born in England, who arrived here by exactly the same route as the rest of us, will rapidly increase. Already by 1985 the native-born would constitute the majority. It is this fact which creates the extreme urgency of action now, of just that kind of action which is hardest for politicians to take, action where the difficulties lie in the present but the evils to be prevented or minimized lie several parliaments ahead.

The natural and rational first question with a nation confronted by such a prospect is to ask: "How can its dimensions be reduced?" Granted it be not wholly preventable, can it be limited, bearing in mind that numbers are of the essence: the significance and consequences of an alien element introduced into a country or population are profoundly different according to whether that element is 1 per cent or 10 per cent.

The answers to the simple and rational question are equally simple and rational: by stopping, or virtually stopping, further inflow, and by promoting the maximum outflow. Both answers are part of the official policy of the Conservative Party.

It almost passes belief that at this moment 20 or 30 additional immigrant children are arriving from overseas in Wolverhampton alone every week—and that means 15 or 20 additional families a decade or two hence. Those whom the gods wish to destroy, they first make mad. We must be mad, literally mad, as a nation to be permitting the annual inflow of some 50,000 dependents, who are for the most part the material of the future growth of the immigrant-descended population. It is like watching a nation busily engaged in heaping up its own funeral pyre. So insane are we that we actually permit unmarried persons to immigrate for the purpose of founding a family with spouses and fiancés whom they have never seen.

Let no one suppose that the flow of dependents will automatically tail off. On the contrary, even at the present admission rate of only 5,000 a year by voucher, there is sufficient for a further 25,000 dependents per annum ad infinitum, without taking into account the huge reservoir of existing relations in this country—and I am making no allowance at all for fraudulent entry. In these circumstances nothing will suffice but that the total inflow for settlement should be reduced at once to negligible proportions, and that the necessary legislative and administrative measures be taken without delay.

I stress the words "for settlement." This has nothing to do with the entry of Commonwealth citizens, any more than of aliens, into this country, for the purposes of study or of improving their qualifications, like (for instance) the Commonwealth doctors who, to the advantage of their own countries, have enabled our hospital service to be expanded faster than would otherwise have been possible. They are not, and never have been, immigrants.

I turn to re-emigration. If all immigration ended tomorrow, the rate of growth of the immigrant and immigrant-descended population would be substantially reduced, but the prospective size of this element in the population would still leave the basic character of the national danger unaffected. This can only be tackled while a considerable proportion of the total still comprises persons who entered this country during the last ten years or so.

Hence the urgency of implementing now the second element of the Conservative Party's policy: the encouragement of re-emigration.

Nobody can make an estimate of the numbers which, with generous assistance, would choose either to return to their countries of origin or to go to other countries anxious to receive the manpower and the skills they represent.

Nobody knows, because no such policy has yet been attempted. I can only say that, even at present,

immigrants in my own constituency from time to
time come to me, asking if I can find them assistance
to return home. If such a policy were adopted and
pursued with the determination which the gravity of
the alternative justifies, the resultant outflow could
appreciably alter the prospects.

The third element of the Conservative Party's
policy is that all who are in this country as citizens
should be equal before the law and that there shall be
no discrimination or difference made between them
by public authority. As Mr Heath has put it, we will
have no "first-class citizens" and "second-class citizens." This does not mean that the immigrant and his
descendent should be elevated into a privileged or
special class or that the citizen should be denied his
right to discriminate in the management of his own
affairs between one fellow-citizen and another or that
he should be subjected to imposition as to his reasons
and motive for behaving in one lawful manner rather
than another.

There could be no grosser misconception of the
realities than that entertained by those who vocifer-
ously demand legislation as they call it "against discrimination," whether they be leader-writers of the
same kidney and sometimes on the same newspapers
which year after year in the 1930s tried to blind this
country to the rising peril which confronted it, or
archbishops who live in palaces, faring delicately with
the bedclothes pulled right up over their heads. They
have got it exactly and diametrically wrong.

The discrimination and the deprivation, the
sense of alarm and of resentment, lies not with the

immigrant population but with those among whom they have come and are still coming.

This is why to enact legislation of the kind before parliament at this moment is to risk throwing a match on to gunpowder. The kindest thing that can be said about those who propose and support it is that they know not what they do.

Nothing is more misleading than comparison between the Commonwealth immigrant in Britain and the American Negro. The Negro population of the United States, which was already in existence before the United States became a nation, started literally as slaves and were later given the franchise and other rights of citizenship, to the exercise of which they have only gradually and still incompletely come. The Commonwealth immigrant came to Britain as a full citizen, to a country which knew no discrimination between one citizen and another, and he entered instantly into the possession of the rights of every citizen, from the vote to free treatment under the National Health Service.

Whatever drawbacks attended the immigrants arose not from the law or from public policy or from administration, but from those personal circumstances and accidents which cause, and always will cause, the fortunes and experience of one man to be different from another's.

But while, to the immigrant, entry to this country was admission to privileges and opportunities eagerly sought, the impact upon the existing population was very different. For reasons which they could not comprehend, and in pursuance of a decision by default, on which they were never consulted, they found themselves made strangers in their own country.

They found their wives unable to obtain hospital beds in childbirth, their children unable to obtain school places, their homes and neighborhoods changed beyond recognition, their plans and prospects for the future defeated; at work they found that employers hesitated to apply to the immigrant worker the standards of discipline and competence required of the native-born worker; they began to hear, as time went by, more and more voices which told them that they were now the unwanted. They now learn that a one-way privilege is to be established by act of parliament; a law which cannot, and is not intended to, operate to protect them or redress their grievances is to be enacted to give the stranger, the disgruntled, and the agent-provocateur the power to pillory them for their private actions.

In the hundreds upon hundreds of letters I received when I last spoke on this subject two or three months ago, there was one striking feature which was largely new and which I find ominous. All Members of Parliament are used to the typical anonymous correspondent; but what surprised and alarmed me was the high proportion of ordinary, decent, sensible people, writing a rational and often well-educated letter, who believed that they had to omit their address because it was dangerous to have committed themselves to paper to a Member of Parliament agreeing with the views I had expressed, and that they would risk penalties or reprisals if they were known to have done so. The sense of being a persecuted minority which is growing among ordinary English people in the areas of the country which are affected is something that those without direct experience can hardly imagine.

I am going to allow just one of those hundreds of people to speak for me:

"Eight years ago in a respectable street in Wolverhampton a house was sold to a Negro. Now only one white (a woman old-age pensioner) lives there. This is her story. She lost her husband and both her sons in the war. So she turned her seven-roomed house, her only asset, into a boarding house. She worked hard and did well, paid off her mortgage, and began to put something by for her old age. Then the immigrants moved in. With grow-ing fear, she saw one house after another taken over. The quiet street became a place of noise and confusion. Regretfully, her white tenants moved out.

"The day after the last one left, she was awakened at 7am by two Negroes who wanted to use her phone to contact their employer. When she refused, as she would have refused any stranger at such an hour, she was abused and feared she would have been attacked but for the chain on her door. Immigrant families have tried to rent rooms in her house, but she always refused. Her little store of money went, and after paying rates, she has less than £2 per week. "She went to apply for a rate reduction and was seen by a young girl, who on hearing she had a seven-roomed house, suggested she should let part of it. When she said the only people she could get were Negroes, the girl said, 'Racial prejudice won't get you anywhere in this country.' So she went home.

"The telephone is her lifeline. Her family pay the bill and help her out as best they can.

*Immigrants have offered to buy her house—at
a price which the prospective landlord would be able
to recover from his tenants in weeks, or at most a few
months. She is becoming afraid to go out. Windows are
broken. She finds excreta pushed through her letter box.
When she goes to the shops, she is followed by children,
charming, wide-grinning piccaninnies. They cannot
speak English, but one word they know. 'Racialist,' they
chant. When the new Race Relations Bill is passed, this
woman is convinced she will go to prison. And is she so
wrong? I begin to wonder."*

The other dangerous delusion from which those
who are willfully or otherwise blind to realities suffer is summed up in the word "integration." To be
integrated into a population means to become for all
practical purposes indistinguishable from its other
members.

Now, at all times, where there are marked physical differences, especially of color, integration is difficult though, over a period, not impossible. There are
among the Commonwealth immigrants who have
come to live here in the last fifteen years or so, many
thousands whose wish and purpose is to be integrated
and whose every thought and endeavor is bent in that
direction.

But to imagine that such a thing enters the heads
of a great and growing majority of immigrants and
their descendants is a ludicrous misconception, and
a dangerous one.

We are on the verge here of a change. Hitherto it has
been force of circumstance and of background which
has rendered the very idea of integration inaccessible

to the greater part of the immigrant population—that they never conceived or intended such a thing, and that their numbers and physical concentration meant the pressures towards integration which normally bear upon any small minority did not operate.

Now we are seeing the growth of positive forces acting against integration, of vested interests in the preservation and sharpening of racial and religious differences, with a view to the exercise of actual domination, first over fellow-immigrants and then over the rest of the population. The cloud no bigger than a man's hand, that can so rapidly overcast the sky, has been visible recently in Wolverhampton and has shown signs of spreading quickly. The words I am about to use, verbatim as they appeared in the local press on 17 February, are not mine, but those of a Labour Member of Parliament who is a minister in the present government:

"The Sikh communities' campaign to maintain customs inappropriate in Britain is much to be regretted. Working in Britain, particularly in the public services, they should be prepared to accept the terms and conditions of their employment. To claim special communal rights (or should one say rites?) leads to a dangerous fragmentation within society. This communalism is a canker; whether practiced by one color or another it is to be strongly condemned."

All credit to John Stonehouse for having had the insight to perceive that, and the courage to say it.

For these dangerous and divisive elements the legislation proposed in the Race Relations Bill is the very pabulum they need to flourish. Here is the means of showing that the immigrant communities can organize to consolidate their members, to agitate and campaign against their fellow citizens, and to overawe and dominate the rest with the legal weapons which the ignorant and the ill-informed have provided. As I look ahead, I am filled with foreboding; like the Roman, I seem to see "the River Tiber foaming with much blood."

That tragic and intractable phenomenon which we watch with horror on the other side of the Atlantic, but which there is interwoven with the history and existence of the States itself, is coming upon us here by our own volition and our own neglect. Indeed, it has all but come. In numerical terms, it will be of American proportions long before the end of the century.

Only resolute and urgent action will avert it even now. Whether there will be the public will to demand and obtain that action, I do not know. All I know is that to see, and not to speak, would be the great betrayal.

Contributors

Renaud Camus

A native of Chamalières in the Auvergne region of central France, Renaud Camus (b. 1946) is one of France's most brilliant stylists and the author of more than 150 books. *Tricks*, until recently the only work by Camus to be translated into English, appeared in 1979 and was prefaced by his mentor, Roland Barthes, one of twentieth-century France's greatest literary critics. In addition to his political writings, an anthology of which, entitled *Enemy of the Disaster*, was published by Vauban Books in 2023, Camus is known for works of fiction, philosophy, travel writing, art criticism, and the extensive diary he has kept and published for over forty years. He lives in the Chateau de Plieux in the village of Plieux in south-western France and is the president of a small political party, the *Party of In-nocence*, which advocates immigration and education reform and the promotion of civic peace.

Ethan Rundell

Ethan Rundell is a translator, journalist, and alumnus of UC, Berkeley, and Paris' School for Advanced Studies in the Social Sciences (EHESS). Rundell has translated over a dozen books as well as scores of academic articles. He lives in North Carolina.

Endnotes

Elegy for Enoch Powell

1 Renaud Camus, *Le Grand Remplacement: Introduction au remplacisme global* (La Nouvelle Librairie, Paris, 2021). First edition, David Reinharc, Neuilly-sur-Seine, 2011.

2 "And all that vomits Subure and Ergastule" [*Et tout ce que vomit Subure et Ergastule*], a line from "Après Cannes," a poem by the Cuban-born French poet José-Maria de Herredia (1842-1905), in his collection, *Les Trophées* (1892). Subure was the most disreputable and densely populated district in ancient Rome, and Ergastule a collection of underground dwellings where slaves and criminals resided.

3 In the original, "*casseurs*" [literally, "breakers"]. Camus is here alluding to a phenomenon that first received notice in February 2006 during demonstrations against a new law regulating first-time employment (le CPE, or *contrat premiere embauche* / First Employment Contract). On several occasions, the protesters, most of whom were high school or university students, were set upon, assaulted, and robbed by groups of black and Arab young people—"*les casseurs*"—who had traveled from the Paris suburbs for this purpose. Partly as a result, the anti-CPE movement fizzled and died. The tactics of "*les casseurs*" would in later years be adopted to different ends by so-called "black bloc" anarchists and other iterations of "antifascist" protestor.

4 The "New Philosophers" refers to a disparate group of French philosophers who broke with Marxism in the 1970s and criticized the political commitments of their predecessors among the post-structuralists. Many went on to occupy a prominent place in the debates of their day, including Pascal Bruckner, Alain Finkielkraut, André Glucksman, and Bernard-Henri Lévy. In some cases—most obviously, that of Bernard-Henri Lévy—their frequent

appearances in the media and obvious taste for the trappings of celebrity exposed them to charges of superficiality and vanity.

The Word "Race"

1   "The worst Limoges, Guantanamos, or Siberias…," all places of banishment, exile, or punishment. "Limoges" here refers to the city of the same name, located in the Haute-Vienne Department of central France. It is the source of the French verb "*limoger*," literally to "to Limoges," which is often used as a semi-humorous synonym for "to dismiss", "relieve of command", or "kick upstairs". The term originates in the practice, during the First World War, of reassigning underperforming senior staff to Limoges—far enough from the front lines that they were unlikely to do further harm.

2   As elsewhere, French public discourse has long been dominated by a "constructivist" understanding of race, according to which race is not (or not primarily) a biological phenomenon but rather a sociological, historical, and political one. Unlike many of its European counterparts, however, and very much unlike the United States, where considerations of race permeate every level of public life, the French state studiously avoids collecting data on the matter, in keeping with a republican commitment to the formal equality of citizens without distinction of "origin, race, or religion" (Constitution of 1958). This makes discussions of race and adjacent concepts particularly fraught, since any mention of the role played by communities of descent or common origin, whether biological or ethnic, may be seen as promoting illegal discrimination and sanctioned accordingly. This particularity of the French context should be kept in mind while reading this essay and the next. See also endnote 15 to the present chapter.

3   The rue Saint-Guillaume in Paris, site of the *École libre des Sciences-Politiques* [Free School of Political Science], subsequently renamed the *Institut d'études politiques de Paris* [Paris Institute of Political Studies], or *Sciences-Po* for short. A prestigious French institution of higher learning and part of the highly selective "grande école" system, it was founded in 1872 as part of an effort to modernize the education of civil servants. Sciences-Po today serves as a major conduit for positions in the French political class and private sector.

4   Frédéric Abadie and Jean-Pierre Corcelette, *Georges Pompidou : Le désir et le destin* (Paris, Éditions Balland, 1994), p. 11.

5   Bernanos, Georges, *La Grande peur des bien-pensants* (Paris, Grasset, 1931), p. 22.

6   George-Alexis Montandon (19 April 1879–30 August 1944) was a Swiss-French anthropologist and proponent of scientific racism prior to World War II. During the German occupation of France, he was responsible for the anti-Semitic exhibition *Le Juif et la France* [The Jew and France] at Paris' Palais Berlitz.

7   An allusion to the entry for "revolution" in the *Nouveau Dictionnaire de la langue française* [New Dictionary of the French Language], first published in 1856 by the French schoolteacher Pierre Larousse, France's answer to Daniel Webster. Now owned by the Hachette publishing group, Larousse remains a major imprint for French-language reference works.

8   Vacher de Lapouge (1854-1936) was a French anthropologist whose racial typology emphasized the superiority of Anglo-Saxon and Nordic peoples to Jews and other European peoples. Lapouge's ideas found favor after his death in Nazi-occupied France. The reference to Chamberlain is to Houston Stewart Chamberlain (1855-1927), a British-German philosopher whose two-volume work *The Foundations of the Nineteenth Century* (1899) influenced the German *Volkische* movement and anti-Semitic racial policy under the Nazi regime. Finally, Camus' reference to Rosenberg is to Alfred Ernst Rosenberg (1893-1946), a Nazi theorist and author of the book, *The Myth of the Twentieth Century* (1930). Rosenberg was executed by hanging in 1946 after being convicted of crimes against humanity at the Nuremberg trials.

9   The French anthropologist and ethnologist Claude Levi-Strauss (1908–2009). The author of a vast body of work, including the memoir *Triste Tropiques* (1955), a foundational text in the genre of autoethnography, Levi-Strauss was a member of the team of geneticists and cultural anthropologists assembled by UNESCO in the wake of the Second World War to draft an official "Statement on Race" (1950). Their finding—principally, that race was little more than a "social myth"—was widely reported in the media. Though the Statement was later revised to accommodate the objections of physical anthropologists, among others, it would go on to supply the basis for a new "constructivist" consensus in discussions of the question. In 1952, UNESCO published Levi-Strauss' contribution to the Statement in pamphlet form ("Race and History"). Levi-Strauss would considerably revise his position in later years, endorsing a form of ethno-differentialism as the condition for cultural creativity and arguing that "cultural diversity and biological diversity are phenomena of the same type." See *60 ans d'histoire de l'UNESCO. Actes du colloque international, Paris 16–18 novembre 2005*, https://sciencespo.hal.science/hal-03569557/

10   Alain Finkielkraut (b. 1949) is a French essayist, public intellectual, and, since 2014, Fellow of the *Académie Française*. Though Finkielkraut is one of Camus' most consistent supporters and agrees with him that the Great Replacement is "not a conspiracy theory," he regrets that the radicality of his friend's positions has made him "totally inaudible" in French debates over immigration and identity. See McCauley, James. 2019. "How Gay Icon Renaud Camus Became the Ideologue of White Supremacy." *The Nation*, 17 June 2019, https://thenation.com/article/archive/renaud-camus-great-replacement-brenton/tarrant/.

11   Simone Veil (1927–2017) was a French magistrate, Holocaust survivor, and politician who served as a minister in several governments and was President of the European Parliament from 1979 to 1982. She is perhaps best remembered for her role as Health Minister, during which time she successfully oversaw a legislative campaign to legalize abortion. A member of the

Académie Française and recipient of the *Légion d'honneur*, Veil was in her life-time widely regarded as a moral authority in public debates. On July 1st, 2018, she was buried at the Panthéon alongside her husband, with French President Emmanuel Macron presiding over the ceremony.

12 *Bathmology, genosuicide, faussel* are all examples of neologisms frequently invoked by Camus. *Bathmology* refers to the "study of levels of language" and was first developed, very much in passing, by Camus' mentor, the French literary critic Roland Barthes. See Barthes' 1975 book, *Roland Barthes par Roland Barthes* (Paris, Seuil, 1975). *Genosuicide* refers to a genocide in which a nation or ethnic group is destroyed by its own hand—a self-willed act of extinction. Camus defines the *faussel* as "the inverted real, the real false, the false real." The term is discussed above in footnote to paage 6, "Elegy for Enoch Powell"

13 Pichot, André. 1996. "Racisme et biologie." Le Monde, 4 October 1996, https://www.lemonde.fr/archives/article/1996/10/04/racisme-et-biologie_3746286_1819218.html

14 See Robert Antelme, *L'Espèce humaine*, (La Cité universelle, Paris, 1947).

15 17th Chamber of the Judicial Court of Paris, responsible for overseeing application of the 1881 law on the freedom of the press. Its remit includes judging accusations of "incitement to racial hatred," which has been a crime in France since 1972. In April 2014, Camus was himself brought before the 17th Chamber after a complaint was filed against him by MRAP, a French antiracist NGO. Camus was found guilty by the court and his sentence upheld on appeal one year later. For the speech that was the object of MRAP's complaint and Camus' closing remarks before the Court, see "*Nocence*, Instrument of the Great Replacement" and "Speech Before the 17th Chamber" in *Enemy of the Disaster: Selected Political Writings of Renaud Camus*, Vauban Books (Blowing Rock, 2023).

16 Émile Maximilien Paul Littré (180–1881), a French lexicographer, freemason, and philosopher best known for his *Dictionnaire de la langue française* (1863-1873), commonly referred to as *le Littré*.

17 Florentine banking family and prominent partners of the Medici. The Cardinal de Retz (1613–1679) was a member of the French branch of the family, which first settled in Lyon in the early sixteenth century.

18 Michel de Montaigne, Les Essais, Chapter XLVI, "Des Noms." The relevant passage reads, in the original: "Pour clorre nostre compte; c'est vn vilain vsage et de tres-mauuaise consequence en nostre France, d'appeller chacun par le nom de sa terre et Seigneurie, et la chose du monde, qui faict plus mesler et mescognoistre les races."

19 See Act V in Jean Baptiste Racine, *Phaedra*, trans. Robert Bruce Boswell, https://www.gutenberg.org/files/1977/1977-h/1977-h.htm

20 The *Grande Larousse* encyclopedia, published in instalments between 1960 and 1964 and last updated in 1975.

21 Chateaubriand, François René de, *Analyse raisonnée de l'histoire de France* (Paris, Librairie de Firmin Didot Frères, 1853), p. 48.

22 A reference to the Loi Haby (Haby Law) of 1975 that was (and still is) criticized for "dumbing down" curricula in the pursuit of equality of outcomes. The term "one middle school" (*college unique*) captures the notion of standardization around a "core curriculum" (*tronc commun*).

23 France Culture is a French public radio station founded in 1963. Its closest American equivalent is NPR.

24 An allusion, apparently, to the poem "Palmes!" by the French poet and diplomat Saint-Jean Perse (Alexis Leger, 1887–1975). Included in the collection, *Éloges* (1910), the poem reads, in part: "*Palmes ! et la douceur d'une vieillesse des racines... ! La terre alors souhaita d'être plus sourde, et le ciel plus profond, où des arbres trop grands, las d'un obscur dessein, nouaient un pacte inextricable...*" (Palms! And the sweetness of age-old roots...! The earth then wished to be more muted, and the sky deeper, where too-large trees, weary with an obscure plan, struck an inextricable pact"). See *Éloges suivi de Gloires des Rois, Anabase, Exil* (Gallimard, Paris, 1960).

25 Marcel Proust, *Cities of the Plain (Sodom and Gommorah)*, vol. 4 of *Remembrance of Things Past*, trans. C.K. Scott Moncrieff (Chatto and Windus, London, 1929), pp. 15–16.

26 Camus here misspells the name of the French journalist and novelist Marc Weitzmann (b. 1959), who played a prominent role in the 2001 Camus Affair. For a full discussion of the Affair and the role played therein by Weitzmann, see Louis Betty's Introduction to *Enemy of the Disaster: Selected Political Writings of Renaud Camus* (Vauban Books, Blowing Rock, 2023).

27 Like their English equivalents, indicated in parentheses, both *nègre* (Negro) and *Mademoisselle* (Miss) have been largely expurgated from contemporary French usage. See note 28 immediately following below.

28 "This prohibition is of the same kind as that forbidding or discouraging use of *Miss*, of the circumflex over *abîme*, and of the past preterit, also judged too discriminating." Camus is here alluding to a series of "reforms," all of which have sought to make French a more inclusive and egalitarian language. As in the English-speaking world, the French term of address for an unmarried woman, *Mademoiselle* (Miss), has been largely eliminated from everyday use in response to concerns that it is paternalistic or otherwise diminishing. In contrast to most accented words in French, the word *abîme* (abyss, gulf) contains an accent (circumflex) that does not inform speakers as to its correct pronunciation; its continued use in written French is thus understood as a form of snobbery, since it may double as a gauge of literacy. The past preterit, finally, is a French verb tense exclusively used in formal contexts to describe past actions that have a definite beginning and end. As with *abîme*, the association of this tense with advanced literacy renders it socially suspect in the eyes of linguistic egalitarians.

29 Jules Michelet, *History of the French Revolution*, trans. Charles Cocks, ed. Gordon Wright (University of Chicago Press, Chicago, 1967), p. 22.

The Deep Murmur

1   Henri Levavasseur, *L'Identité, socle de la cité. Réconcilier ethnos et polis* (La Nouvelle Librairie, Paris, 2021).

2   Renaud Camus, *Dictionnaire des délicatesses du français contemporain*, 2 vols. (Editions du Château, Plieux, 2021).

3   Camus is here alluding to a famous 1959 letter from Charles de Gaulle to his confidant Alain Peyrefitte, in which De Gaulle argues for granting independence to French Algeria: "It is good that there are yellow Frenchmen, black Frenchmen, and brown Frenchmen. They show that France is open to all races and has a universal calling. But only on the condition that they stay a small minority. If not, France will no longer be France. In the end, we remain a European people of the white race, Greek and Latin culture, and Christian religion…"

4   "Regroupement familial," or "family reunification," is an administrative measure established by decree in 1978 that permits lawfully resident foreigners to be joined on French soil by their family members. As elsewhere, this measure accounts for a significant proportion of the total immigration flow to France (according to INED, the French national institute of demography, fully 41% of legal immigration to the country was due to family reunification in 2019, the last year for which statistics are available) and has been a source of controversy ever since it was adopted. For the "Haby Law" and the "one middle school" system, see "The Word 'Race'", endnote 22 above.

5   "*… pardon, des médias de l'égout central, négationniste-génocidaire.*" A depreciative play on words. Camus is here alluding to the English phrase, "mainstream media," which he employs without translation immediately beforehand. His "sorry, the *sewage stream*, genocidal negationist media" should be understood as commentary on that phrase's implicit analogy with the prevailing current of a body of water: consensus opinion is indeed like the prevailing current of a body of water, he is suggesting, but that body of water is a sewer, containing only filth (*l'égout central* = central sewer).

6   In January 2016, a new administrative map was adopted for metropolitan France. In place of the 22 regions inherited from the French Revolution, which had themselves replaced the roughly three dozen provinces recognized under the Old Regime, 12 new regions were created. Amalgamated from bits and pieces of their predecessors, and with little regard for history, tradition, or geographical continuity, these new regions have been widely criticized for their arbitrary, Frankenstein-like character.

Also available from Vauban Books

Renaud Camus, *Enemy of the Disaster: Selected Political Writings of Renaud Camus,* with an Introduction by Louis Betty (2023)